EASY PIANO

12 TOP HITS

ISBN 0-7935-8437-X

7777 W. BLUEMOUND RD. P.O. BOX 13819 MILWAUKEE, WI 53213

Visit Hal Leonard Online at
www.halleonard.com

EASY PIANO

12 TOP HITS

CONTENTS

ALL BY MYSELF

Music by SERGEI RACHMANINOFF
Words and Additional Music by ERIC CARMEN

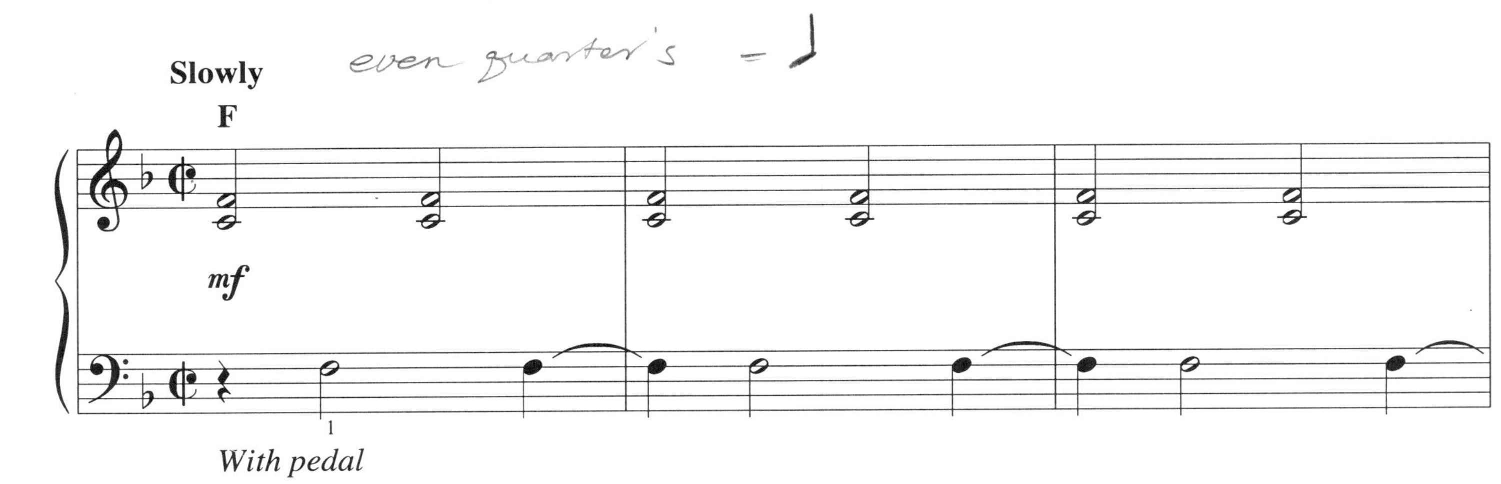

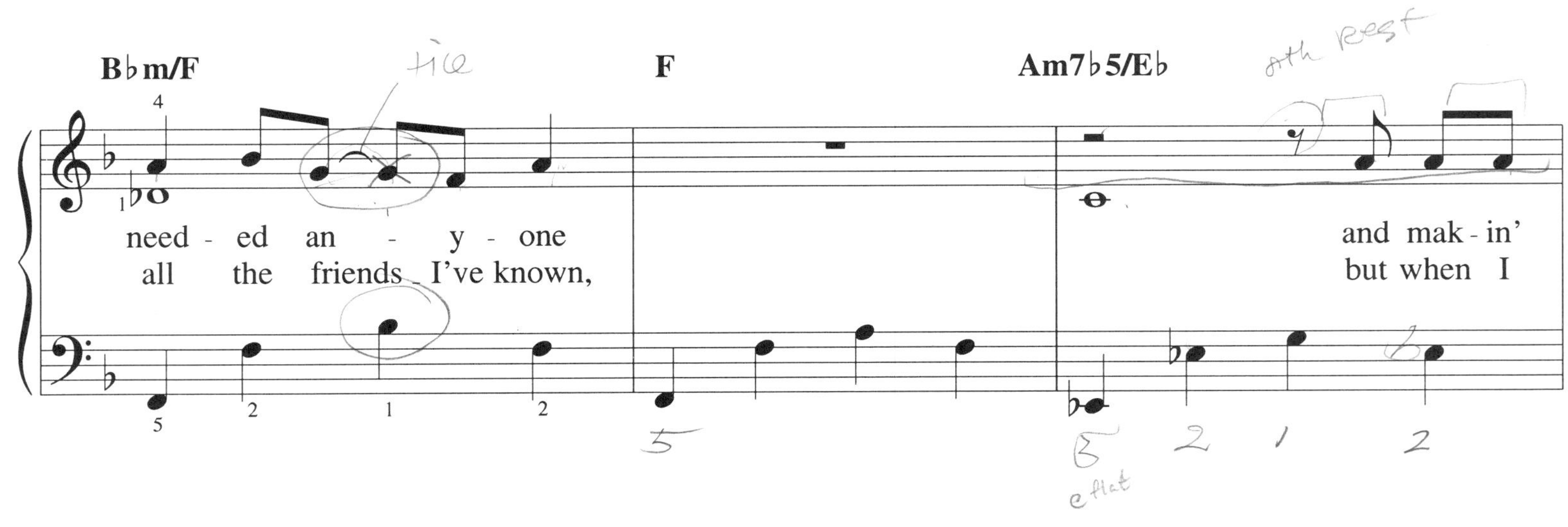

Dsus
D
Gm
B♭m6
love was just for fun;
dial the tel - e-phone
those days are gone.
no-bod - y's home.
F/A
1.
Gm7♭5
C7/E
2.
F/A
D7
G7
Gm7♭5/D♭
C7
F
Am
All by my - self,

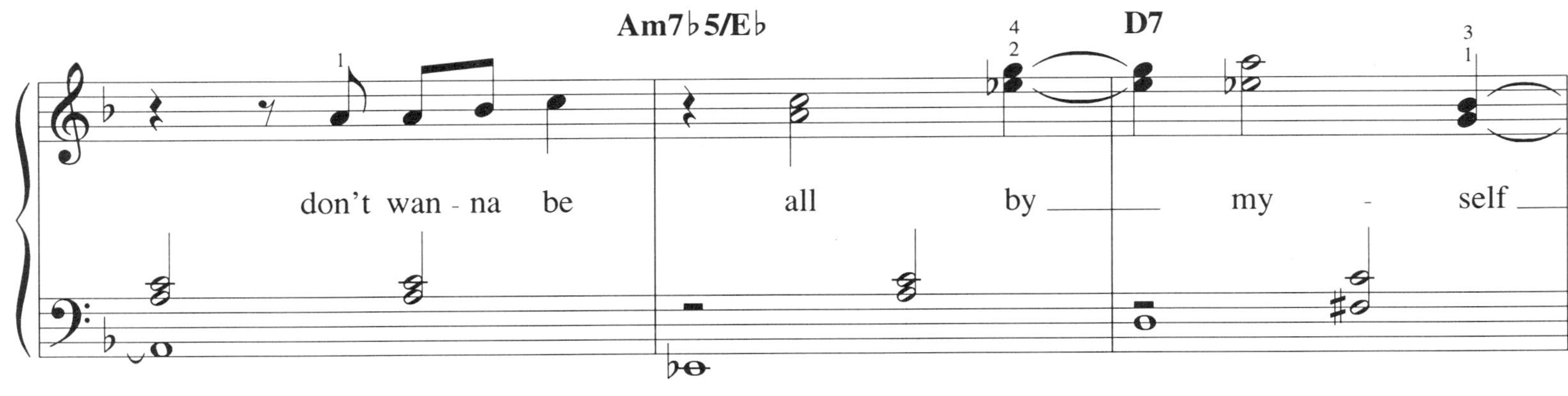
Am7♭5/E♭
D7
don't wan - na be
all
by
my
-
self

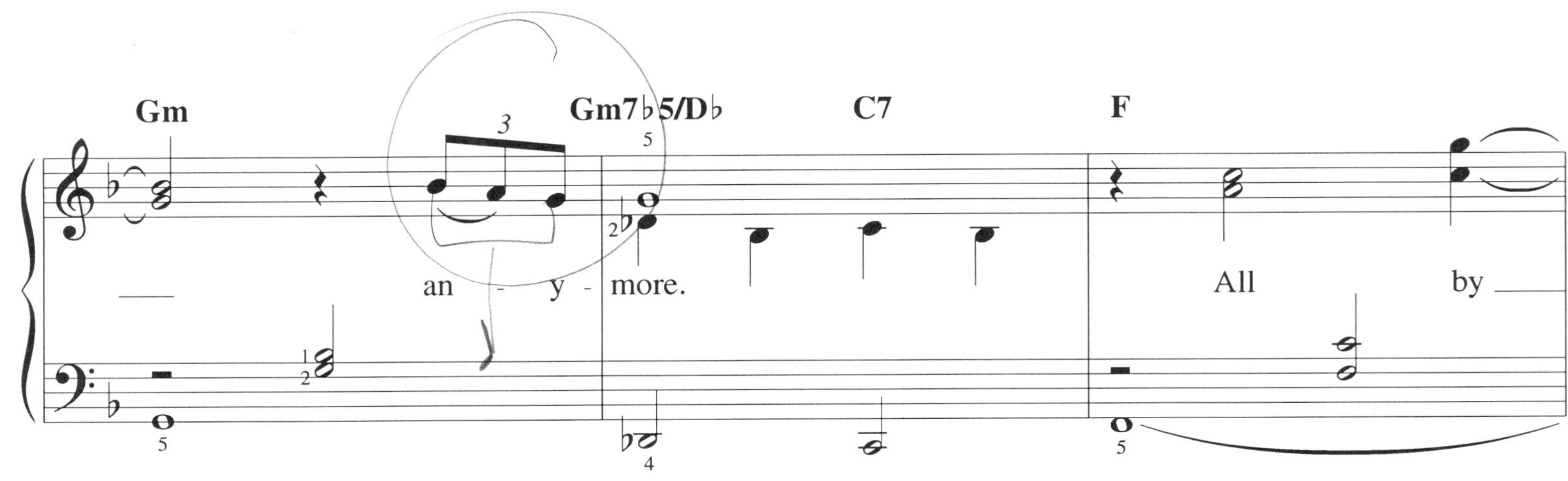
Gm
Gm7♭5/D♭
C7
F
an
-
y
-
more.
All
by

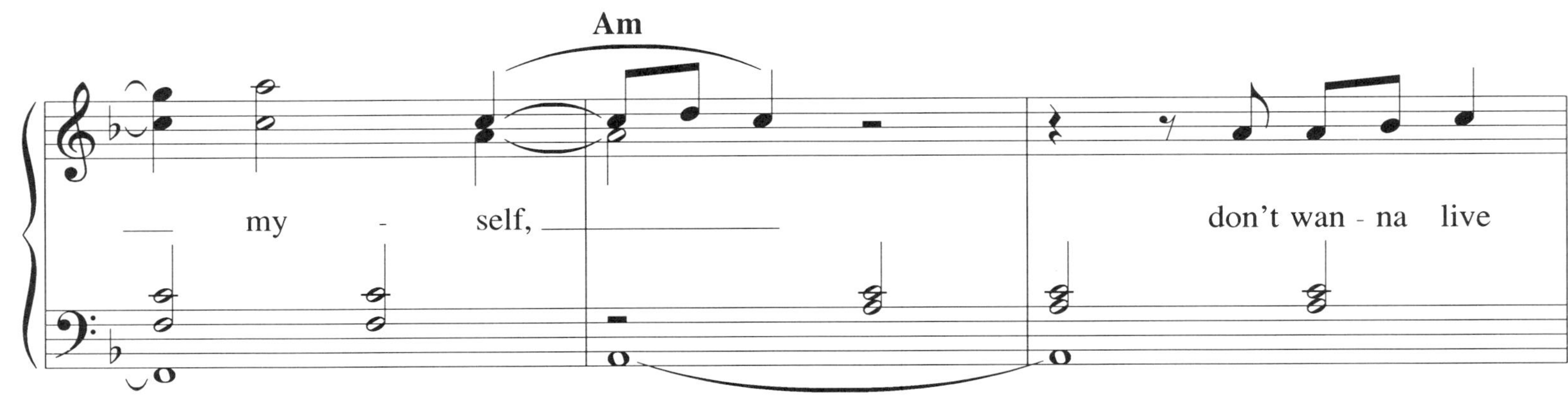
Am
my
-
self,
don't wan - na live

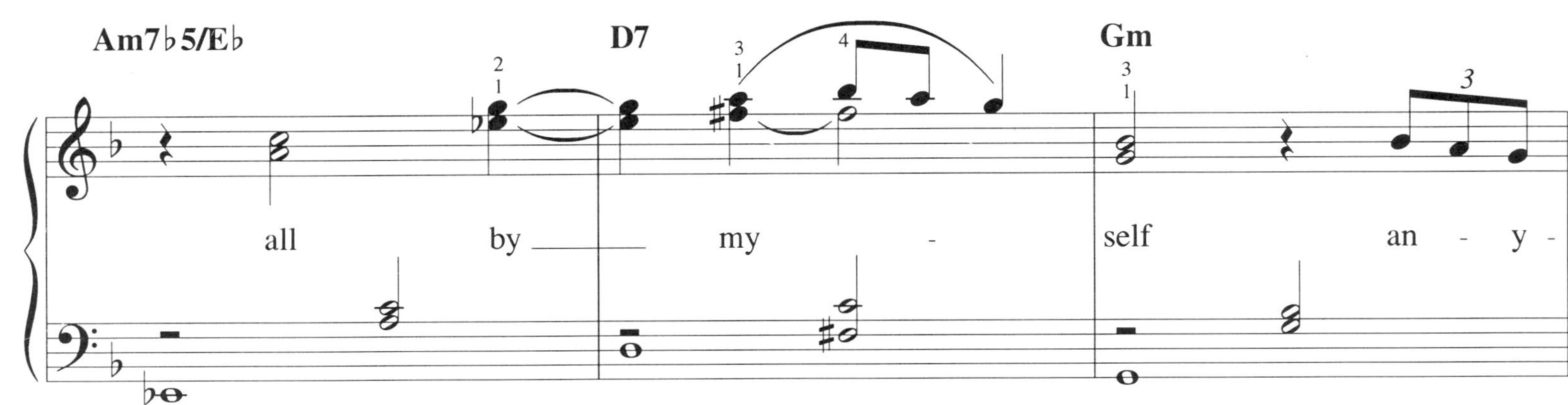
Am7♭5/E♭
D7
Gm
all
by
my
-
self
an
-
y
-

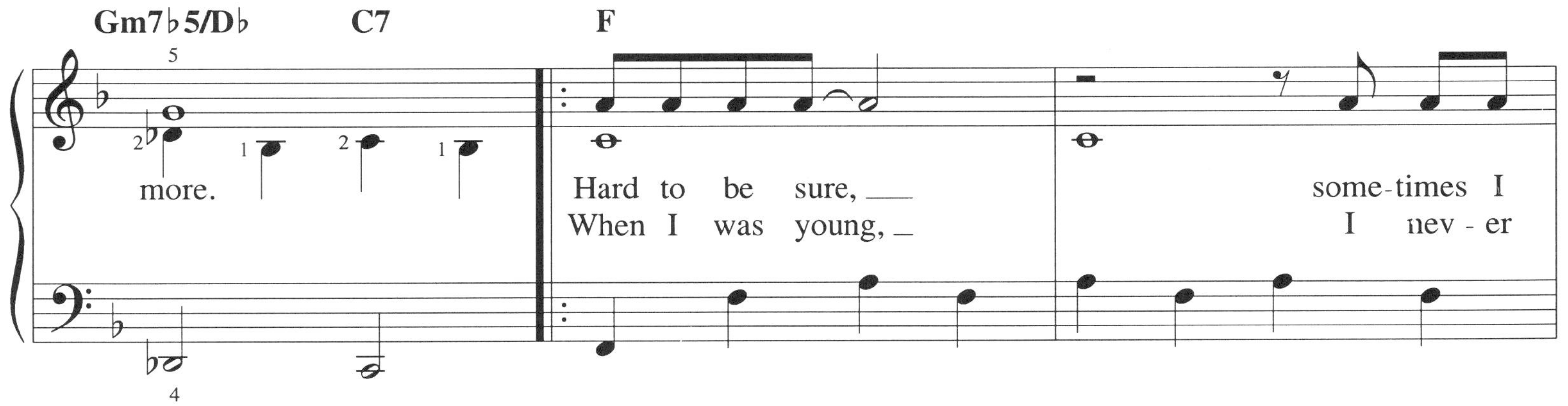
Gm7♭5/D♭
C7
F
more.
Hard to be sure,
sometimes I
When I was young,
I nev-er

B♭m/F
F
Am7♭5/E♭
feel so in-se-cure,
and love so
need-ed an-y-one,
and ma-kin'

Dsus
D
Gm
B♭m6
1.
F/A
dis-tant and ob-scure
re-mains the cure.
love was just for fun;
those days are gone.

Gm7♭5
C/E
2.
F/A
Gm7♭5
C/E
F

DON'T CRY FOR ME ARGENTINA

from EVITA

Words by TIM RICE
Music by ANDREW LLOYD WEBBER

G/B
D7
G
nines at six - es and sev - ens with you.

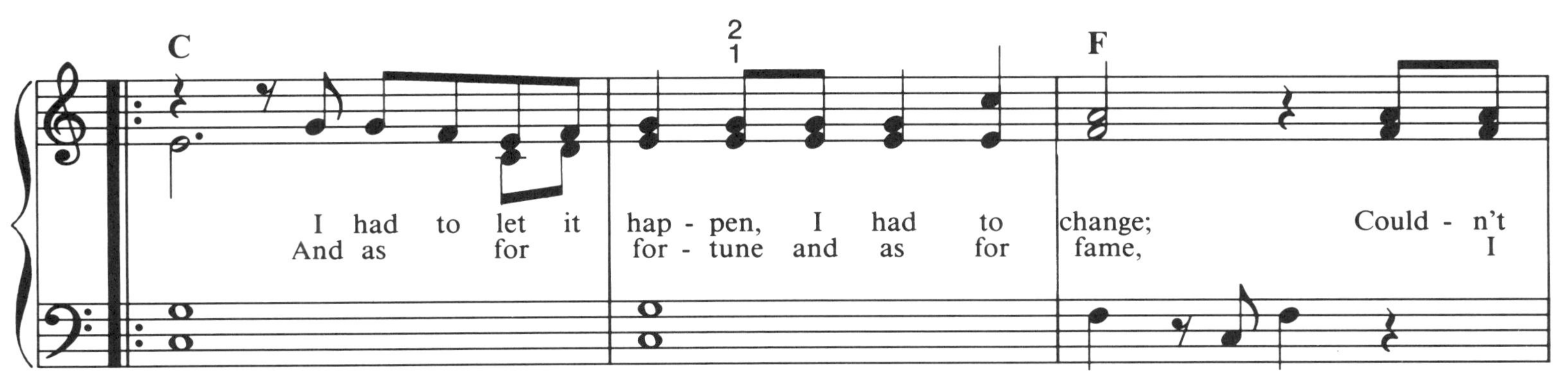
C
F
I had to let it hap - pen, I had to change; Could - n't
And as for for - tune and as for fame, I

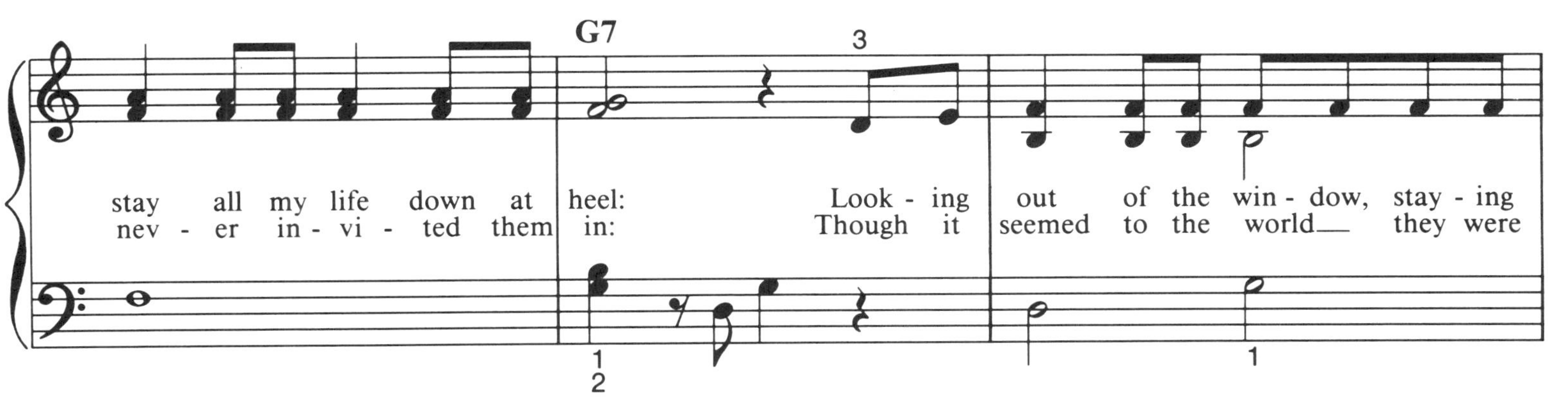
G7
stay all my life down at heel: Look - ing out of the win - dow, stay - ing
nev - er in - vi - ted them in: Though it seemed to the world they were

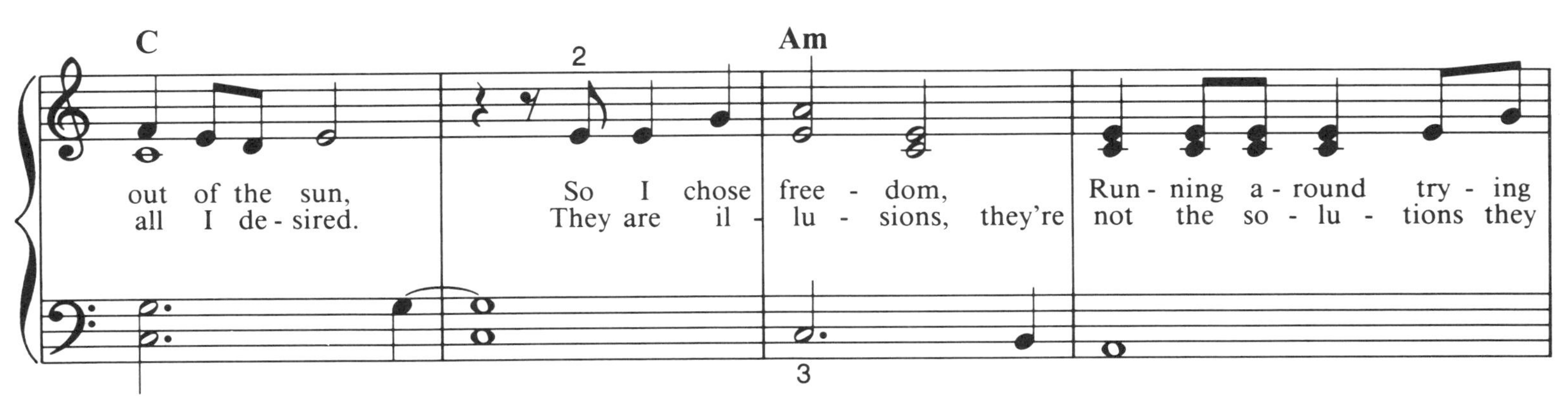
C
Am
out of the sun, So I chose free - dom, Run - ning a - round try - ing
all I de - sired. They are il - lu - sions, they're not the so - lu - tions they

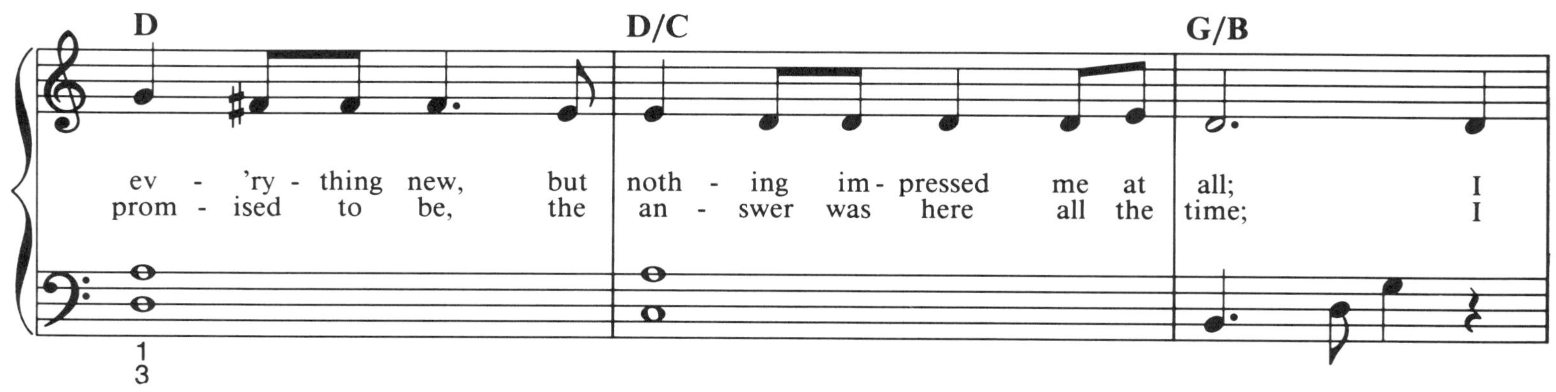
D
D/C
G/B
ev - 'ry - thing new, but noth - ing im - pressed me at all; I
prom - ised to be, the an - swer was here all the time; I

D7
G
C
nev - er ex - pect - ed it to.
love you and hope you love me,
Don't cry for me Ar - gen -

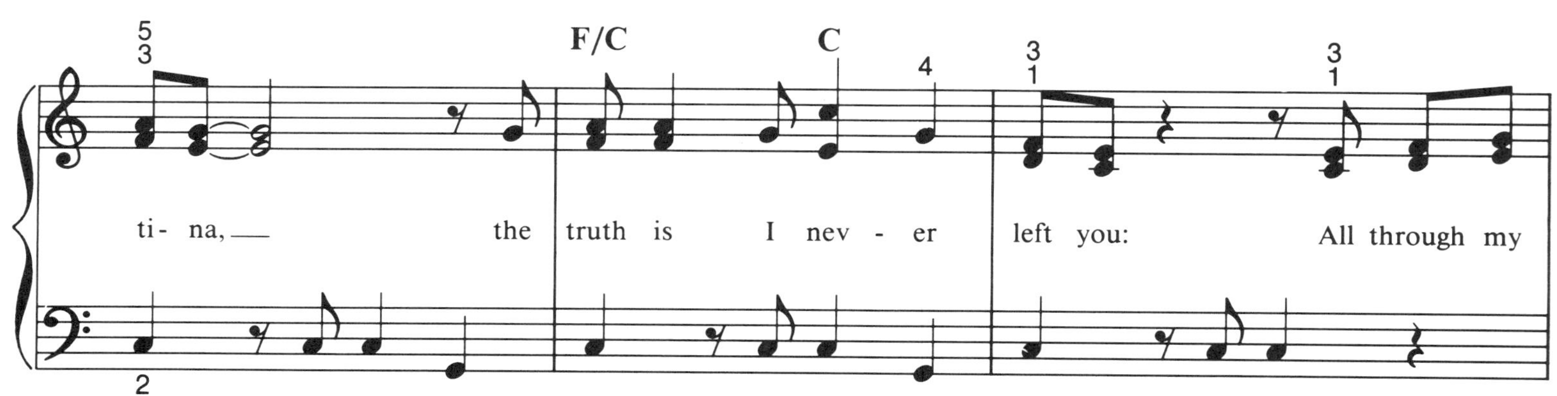
F/C
C
ti - na, the truth is I nev - er left you: All through my

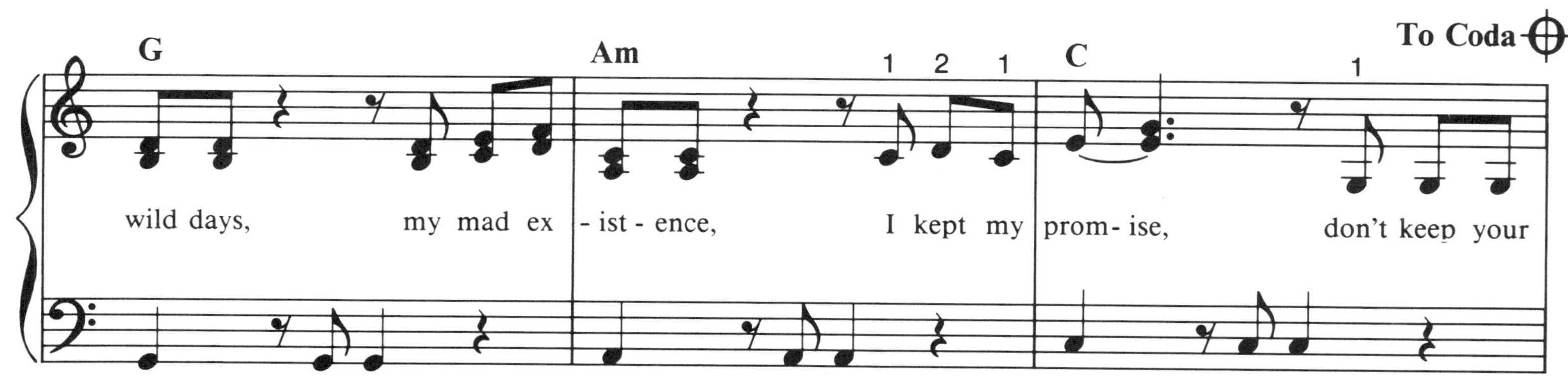
G
Am
C
To Coda
wild days, my mad ex - ist - ence, I kept my prom - ise, don't keep your

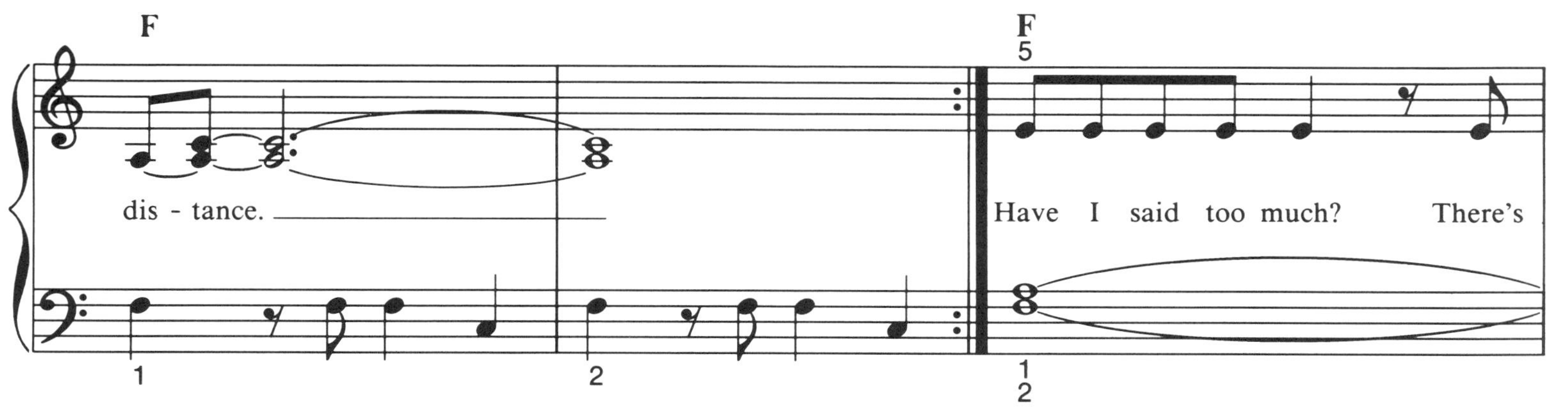
F
F
5
dis - tance.
Have I said too much? There's
1
2
1
2

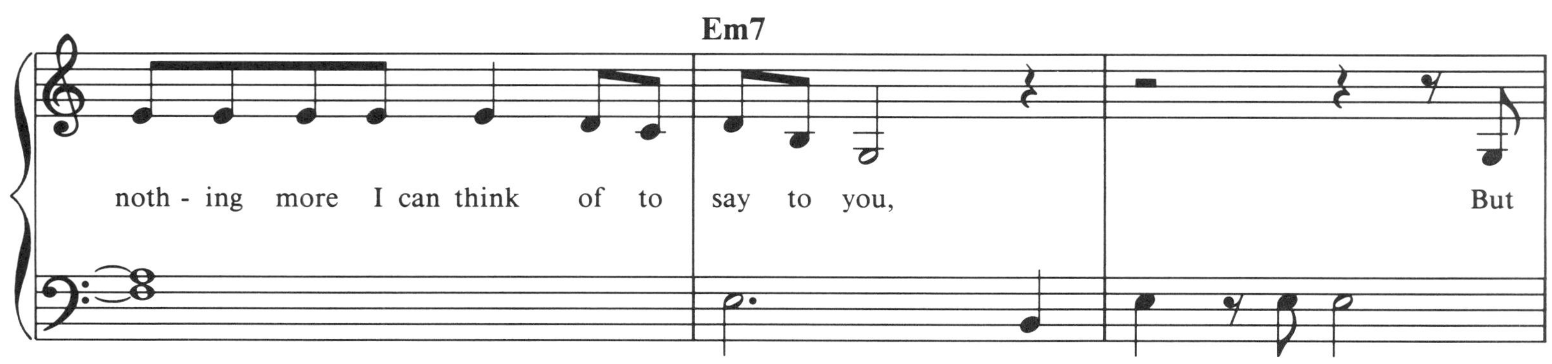
Em7
noth - ing more I can think of to say to you,
But

Fmaj7
4
C
2
D.S. al Coda
all you have to do is look at me to know that ev - 'ry word is true.

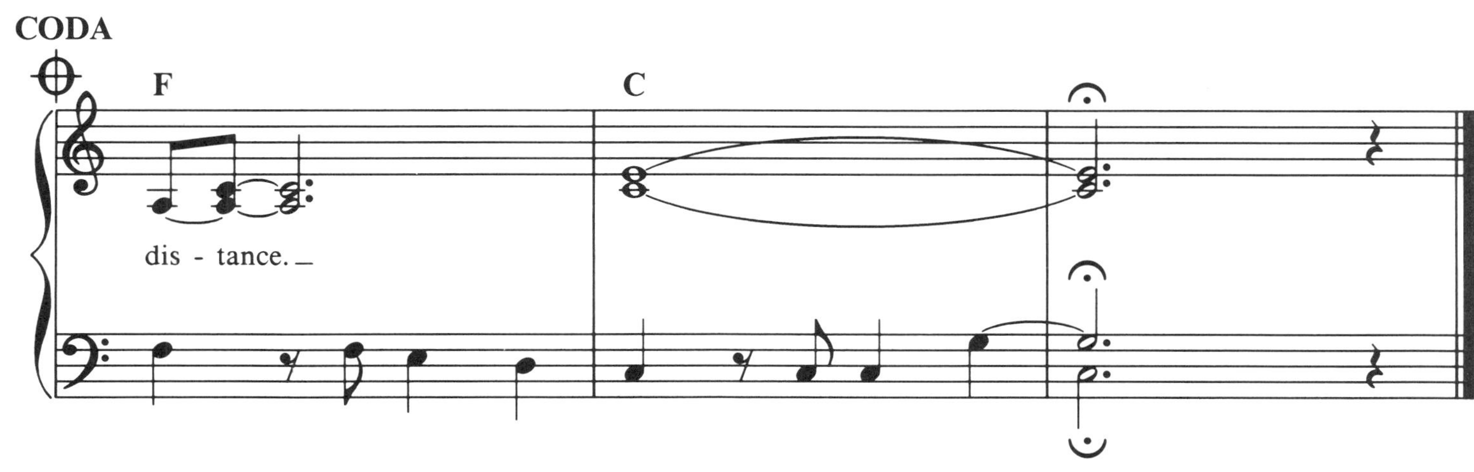
CODA
F
C
dis - tance.

EVERYTIME I CLOSE MY EYES

Words and Music by
BABYFACE

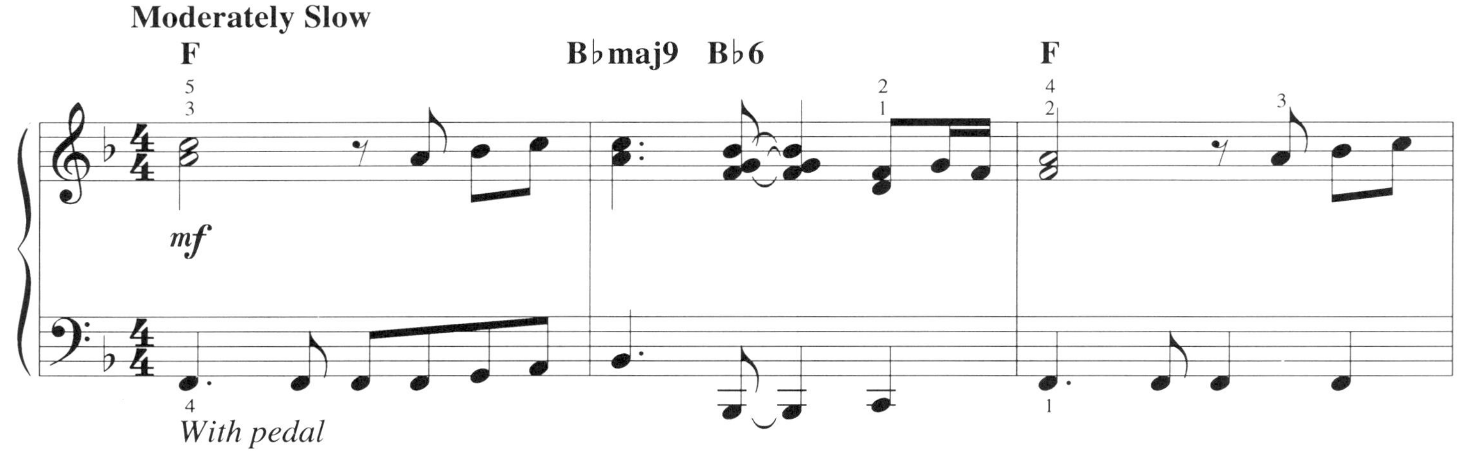

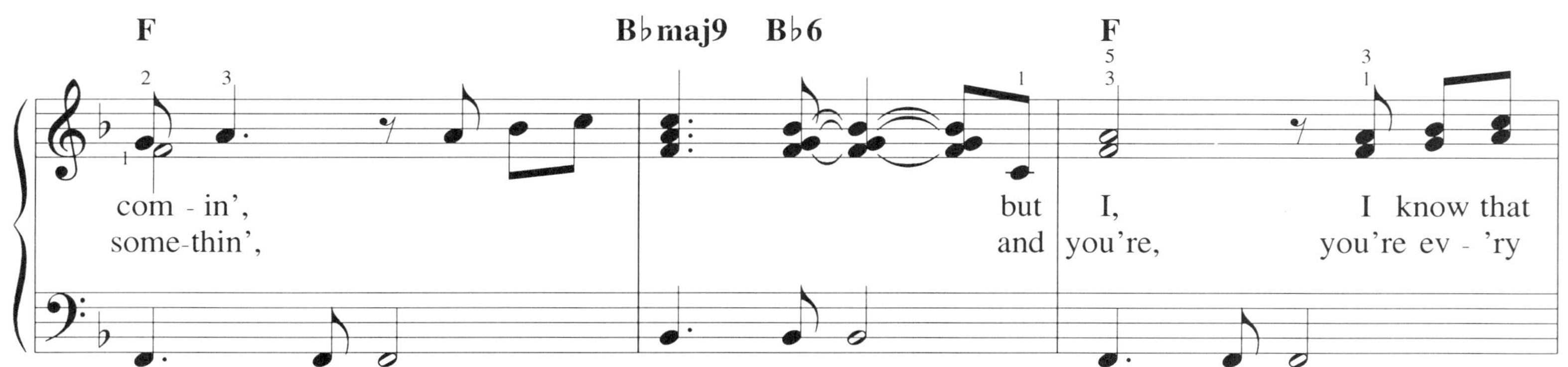

B♭maj9
B♭6
F
B♭maj9
B♭6
it's been worth the wait.
Yeah.
bit of a dream come true.
With

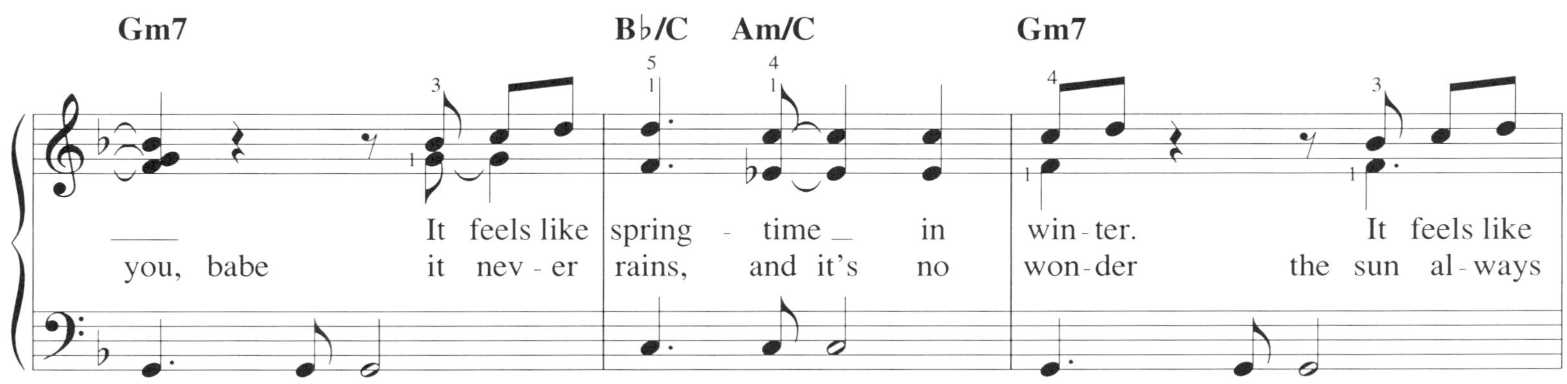
Gm7
B♭/C
Am/C
Gm7
It feels like spring - time in win - ter. It feels like
you, babe it nev - er rains, and it's no won - der the sun al - ways

B♭/C
Am/C
C/B♭
Am7
Am7/D
A♭13♭5
Christ - mas in June. It feels like heav - en has
shines when I'm near you. It's just a bless - ing that

Gm7
Am7
B♭/C
F
Am/E
o - pened up its gates for me and you.
I have found some - bod - y like you.
And
ev - 'ry - time I close my eyes, I

Dm
F/C
B♭maj9
B♭/C
thank the Lord that I've got you and you've got me, too. And
F
Am/E
Dm
F/C
B♭maj9
To Coda
ev - 'ry-time I think of it, I pinch my-self 'cause I don't be - lieve it's true that
1.
C9
C7sus
F
B♭maj9
B♭6
some-one like you loves me too.
F
D♭maj9
Gm7/C
2.
Gm7/C
C7
some-one like you loves me too.

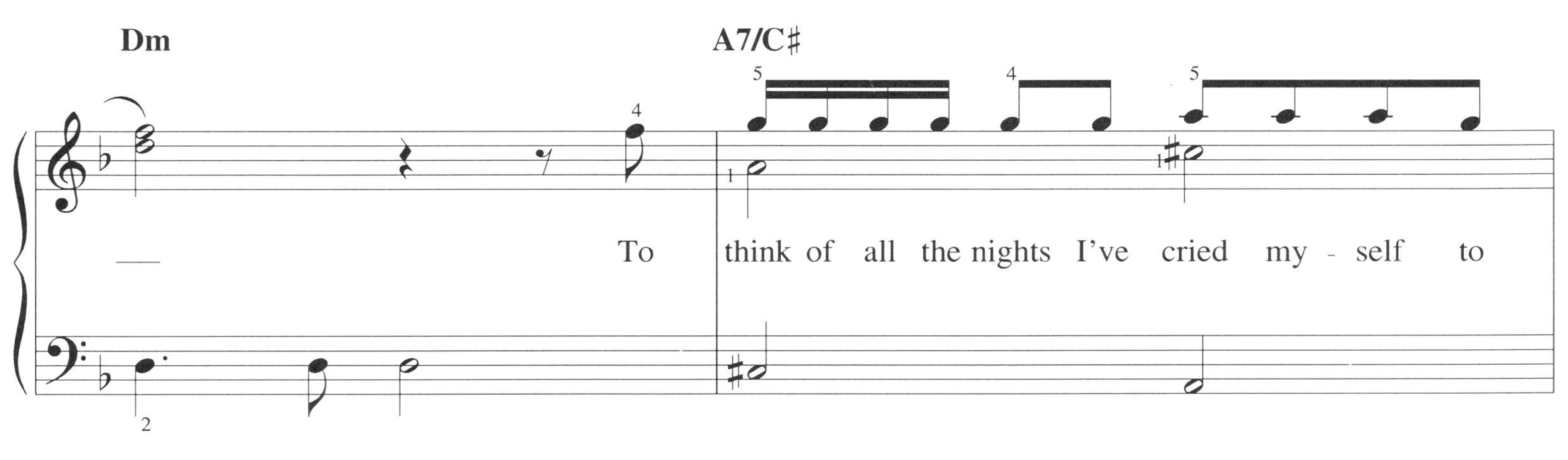
Dm
A7/C♯
To
think of all the nights I've cried my - self to

F/C
G7/B
sleep.
You
real - ly ought - a know how much you mean to

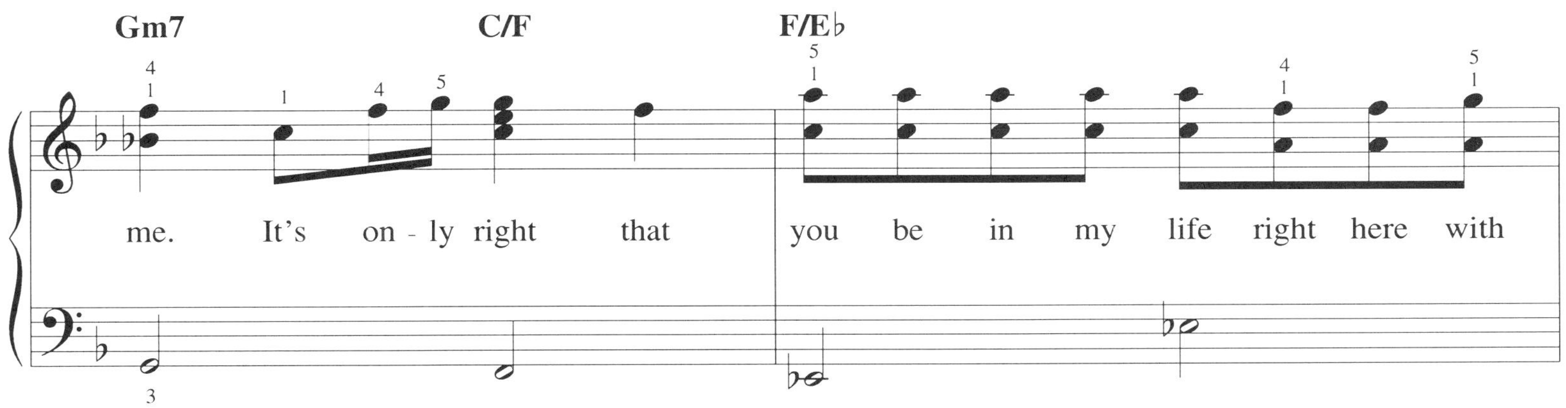
Gm7
C/F
F/E♭
me. It's on - ly right that
you be in my life right here with

B♭maj7/C
F
Am7/E
me. Oh, ba - by, ba - by,
yeah.

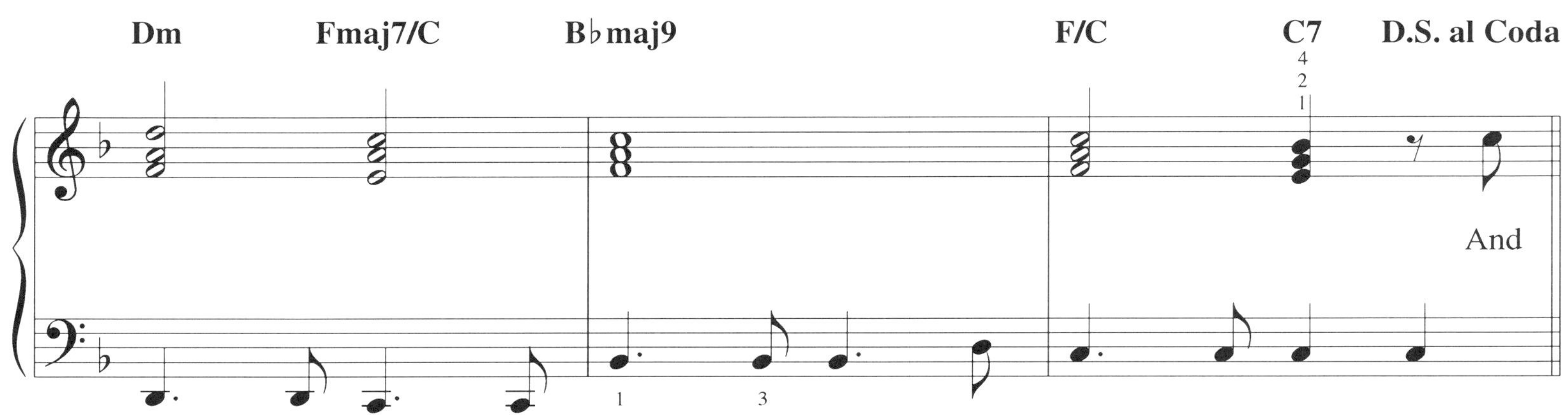
Dm
Fmaj7/C
B♭maj9
F/C
C7
D.S. al Coda
And

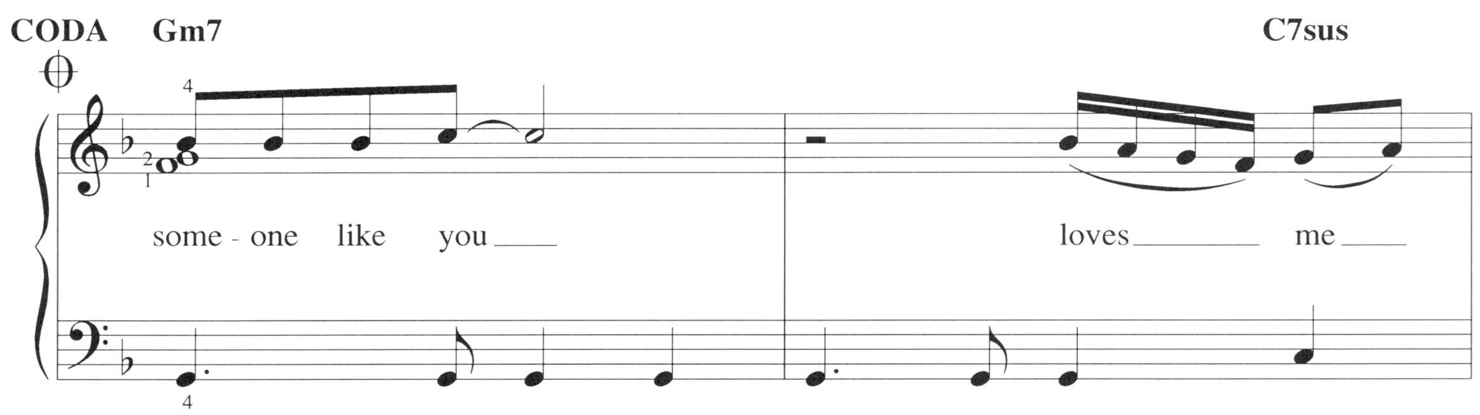
CODA
Gm7
C7sus
some - one like you
loves me

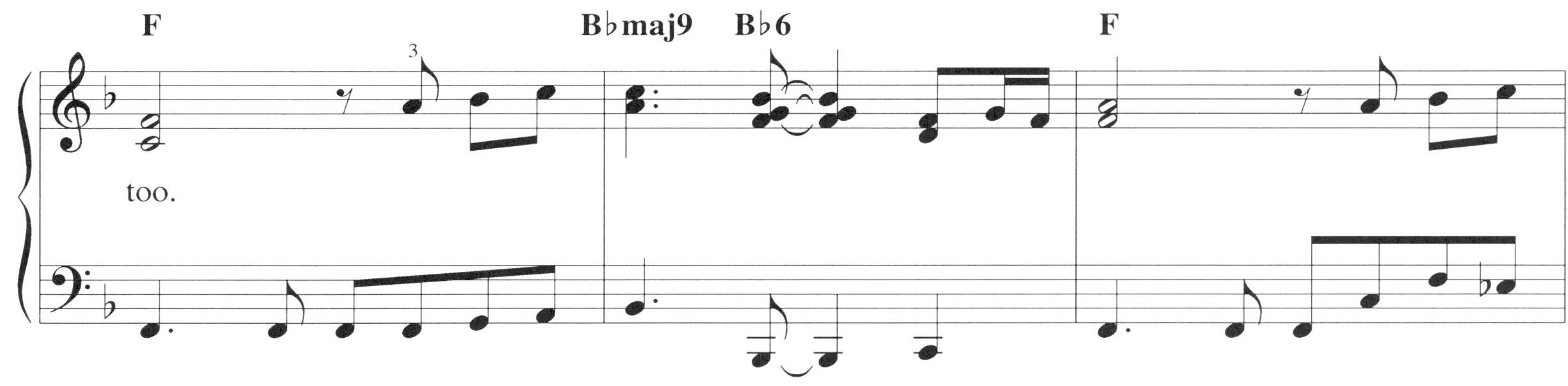
F
B♭maj9
B♭6
F
too.

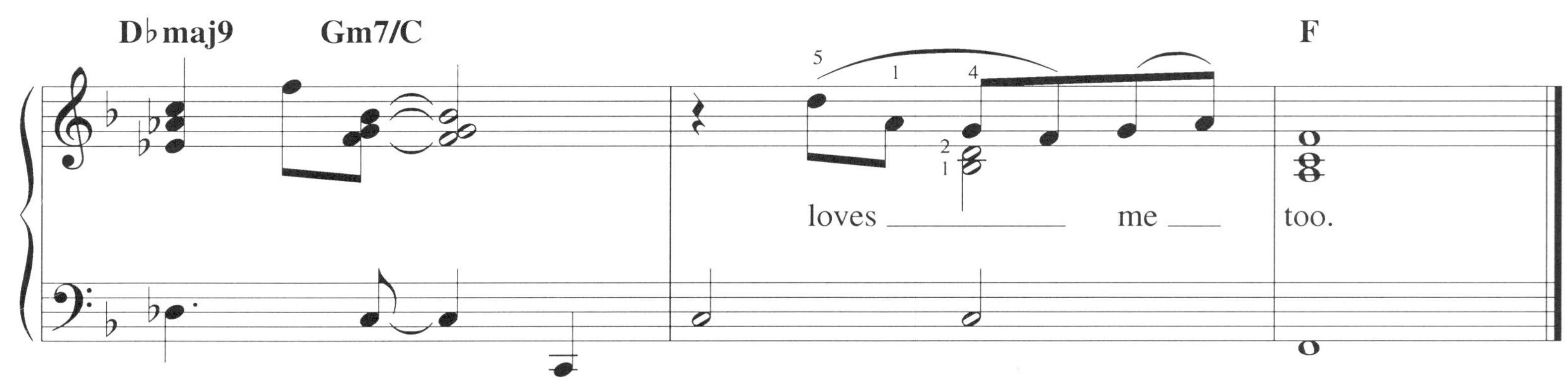
D♭maj9
Gm7/C
F
loves me
too.

I BELIEVE IN YOU AND ME

from the Touchstone Motion Picture THE PREACHER'S WIFE

Words and Music by DAVID WOLFERT
and SANDY LINZER

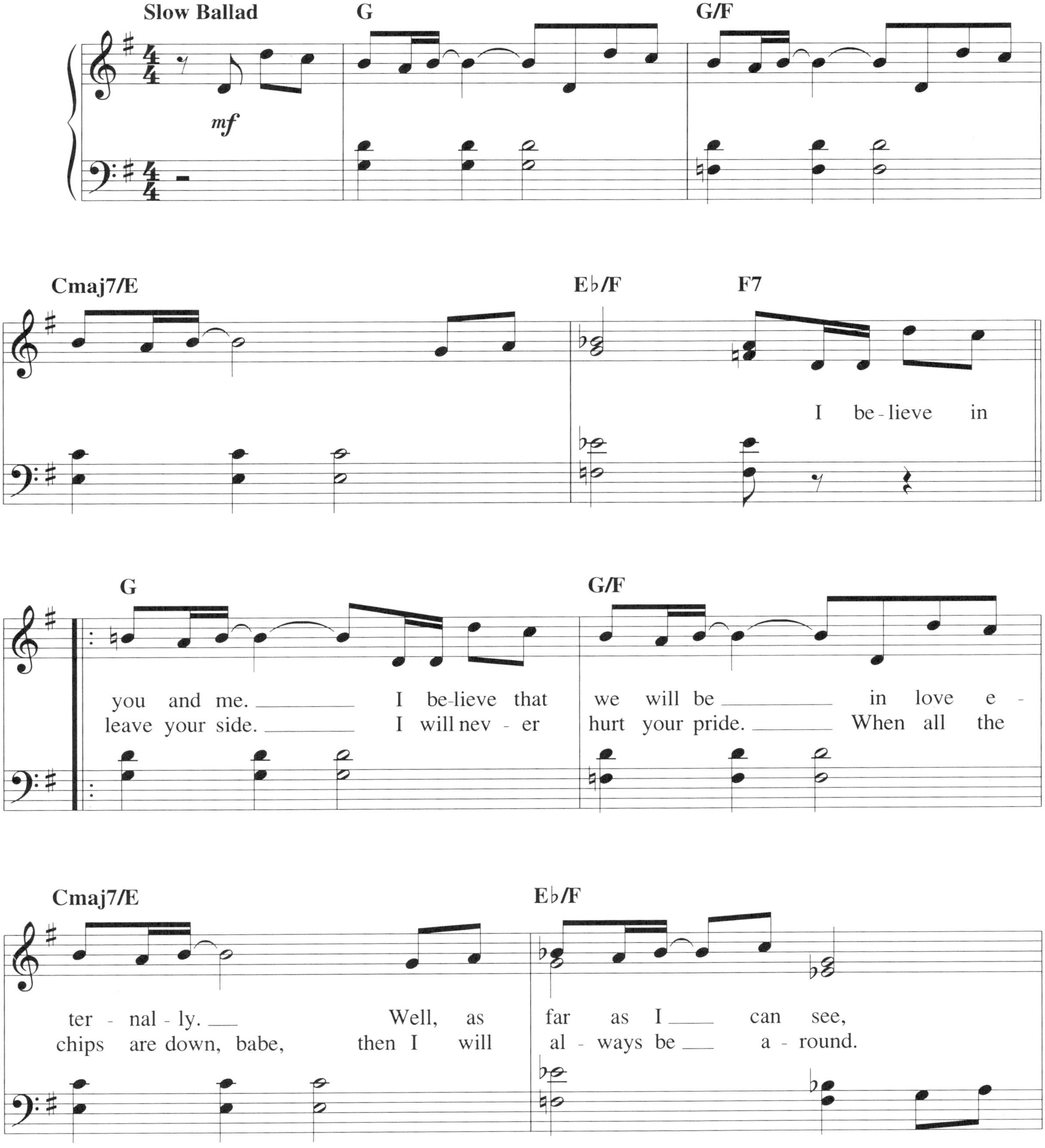
Slow Ballad
G
G/F
mf
Cmaj7/E
E♭/F
F7
I be - lieve in
G
G/F
you and me. ___ I be-lieve that we will be ___ in love e -
leave your side. ___ I will nev - er hurt your pride. ___ When all the
Cmaj7/E
E♭/F
ter - nal - ly. ___ Well, as far as I ___ can see,
chips are down, babe, then I will al - ways be ___ a - round.

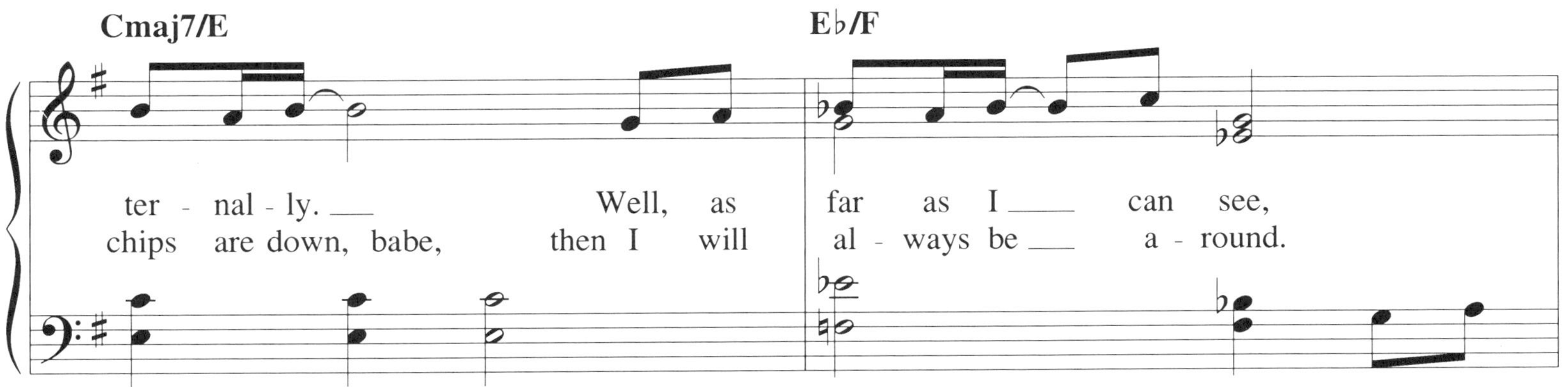

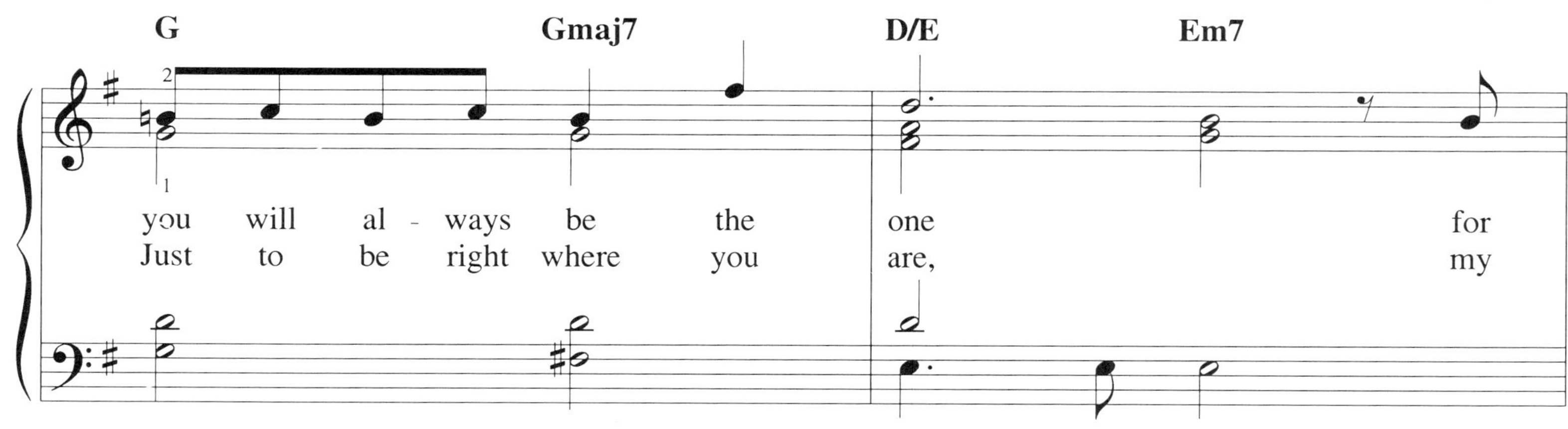
G
Gmaj7
D/E
Em7
you will al - ways be the one for
Just to be right where you are, my

Bm7
Am7
D7sus
me. Oh, yes, you will. And I be-lieve in
love. You know I love you, boy. I'll nev - er

G
G/F
dreams a - gain. I be-lieve that love will nev - er end. And
leave you out. I will al - ways let you in, boy oh ba-by, to

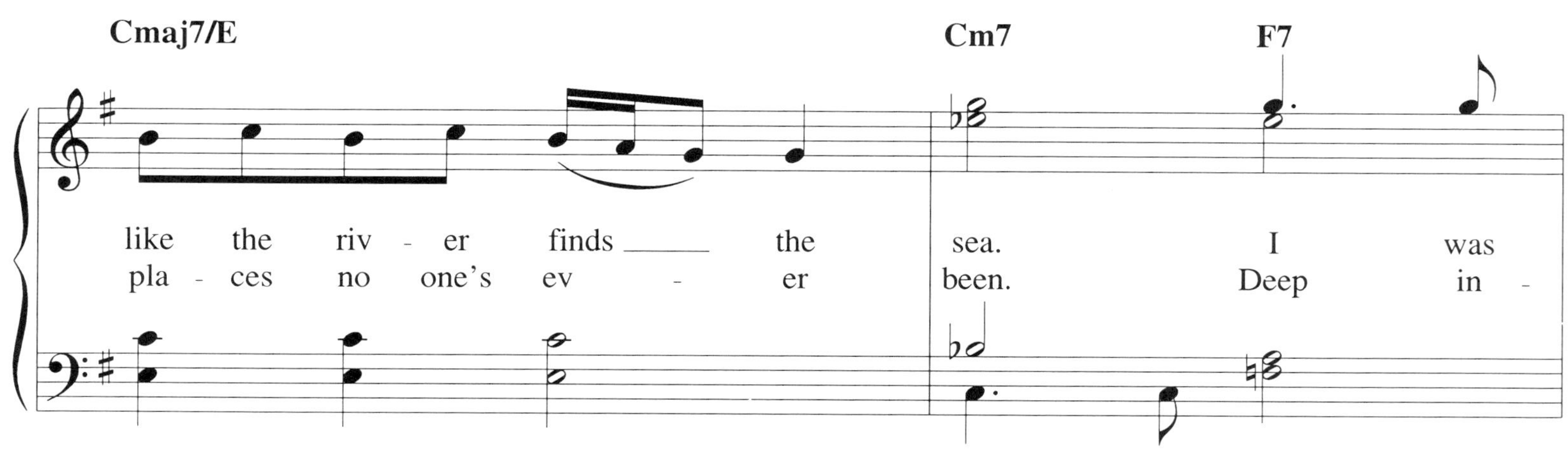
Cmaj7/E
Cm7
F7
like the riv - er finds the sea. I was
pla - ces no one's ev - er been. Deep in -

G/D
Bm7
Em7
lost, now I'm
free 'cause
side, can't you
see that
Am7
C/D
1.
G
C/D N.C.
I be - lieve in you and
me. I will nev - er
I be - lieve in you and
2.
G
Bm7
Em7
4
me.
May - be I'm a fool to
Bm7
Em7
Am
Am(maj7) Am7
feel the way I do.
I would play the fool for - ev - er

D7sus
just to be with you for - ev - er.
I be-lieve in

G
G/F
mir - a - cles, and love's a
mir - a - cle, and yes,

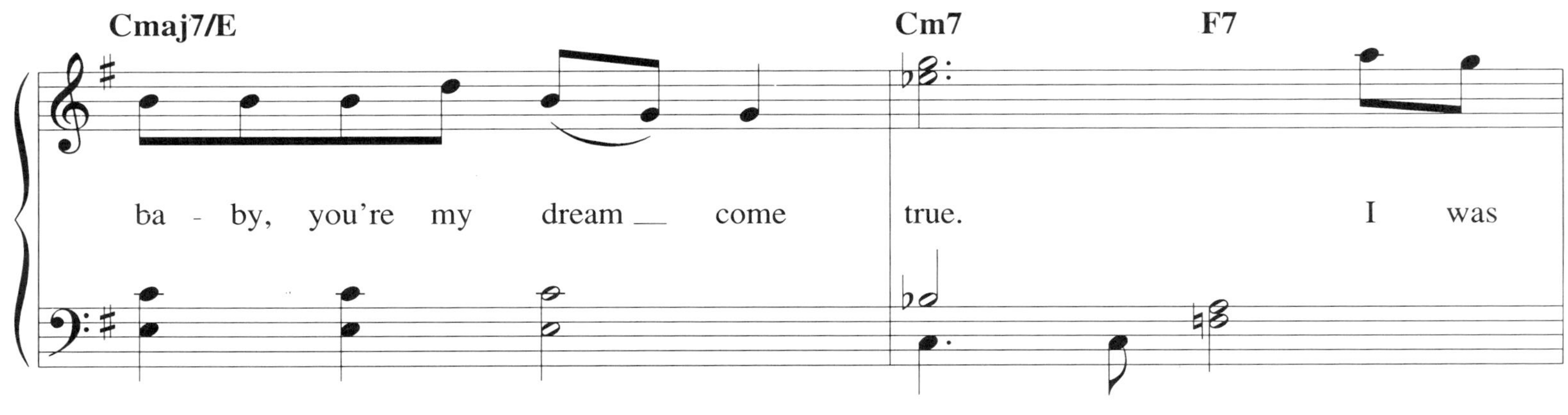
Cmaj7/E
Cm7
F7
ba - by, you're my dream come
true. I was

G/D
Bm7
Em7
lost, now I'm
free, oh ba - by, 'cause

Am7
D7sus
F/G
G/B
I be - lieve, I do be - lieve in you and me. See, I'm

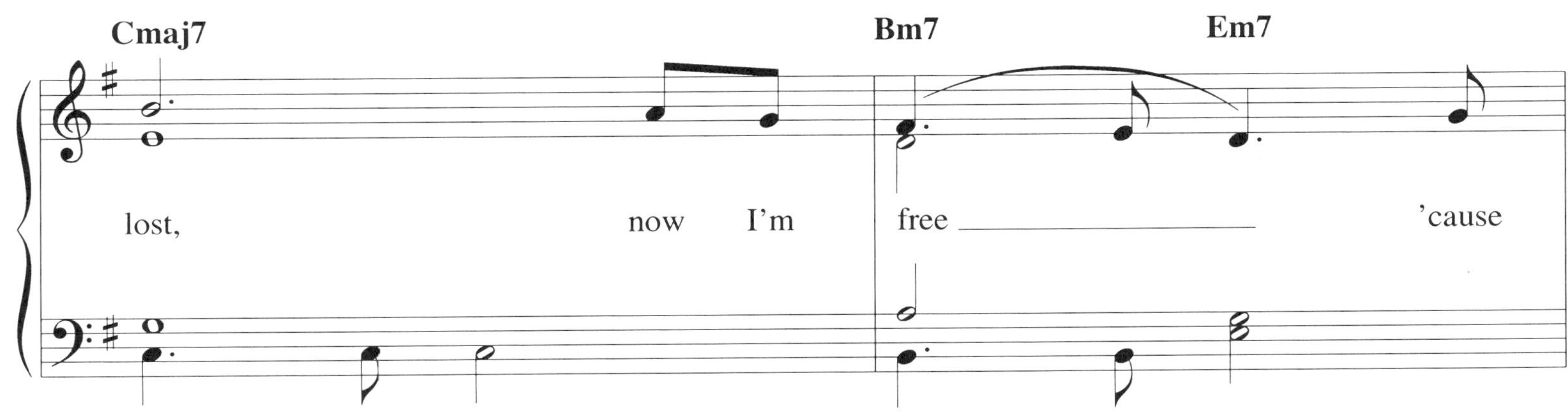
Cmaj7
Bm7
Em7
lost, now I'm free 'cause

Am7
C/D
N.C.
G
I be-lieve in you and me.

G/F
Cmaj7
Am7
D7sus
G(add9)

FOR THE FIRST TIME

Words and Music by ALLAN RICH,
JAMES NEWTON HOWARD and JUD FRIEDMAN

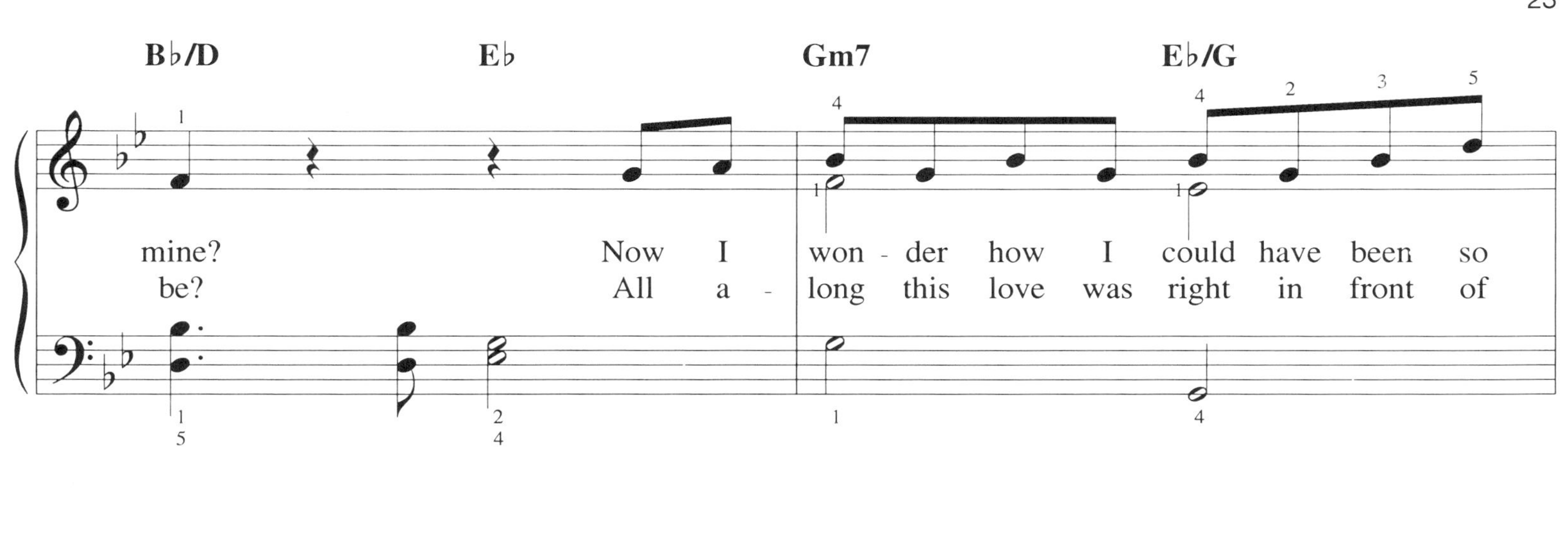
B♭/D
E♭
Gm7
E♭/G
mine? Now I won - der how I could have been so
be? All a - long this love was right in front of

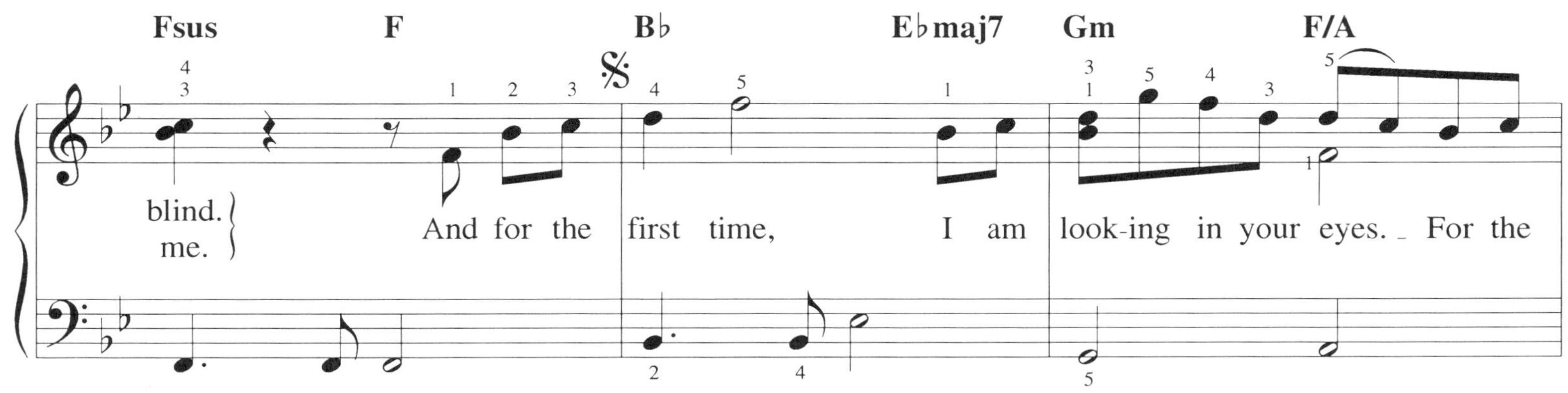
Fsus
F
B♭
E♭maj7
Gm
F/A
blind.
me.
And for the first time, I am look-ing in your eyes. For the

B♭
E♭
Fsus
F
first time I'm see-ing who you are. I can't be -

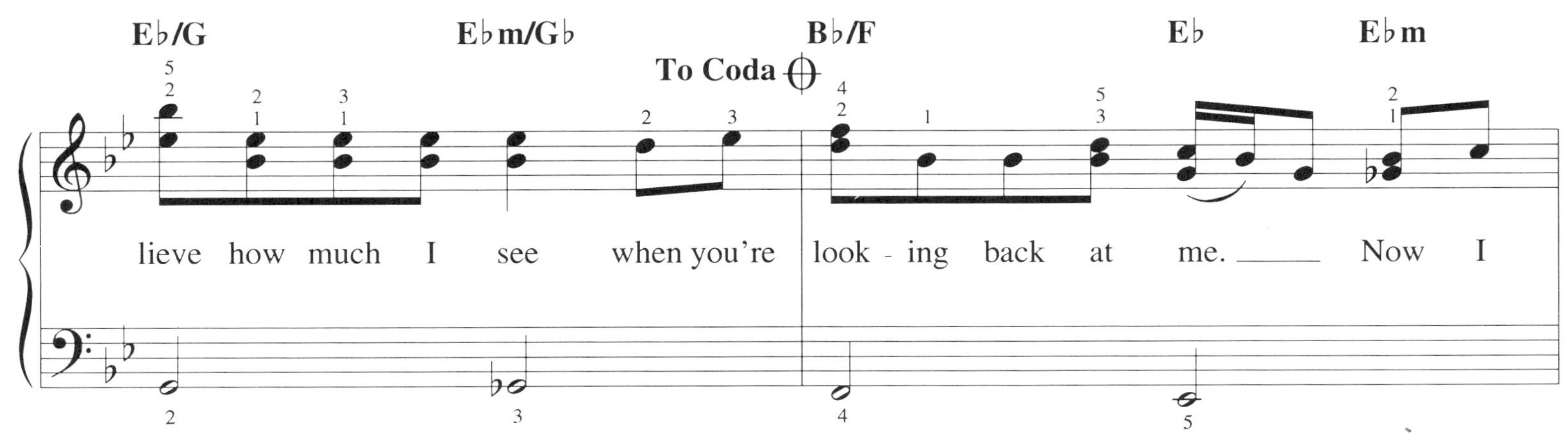
E♭/G
E♭m/G♭
To Coda
B♭/F
E♭
E♭m
lieve how much I see when you're look - ing back at me. Now I

B♭/F
Gm
Cm7
F
1.
B♭
Gm
un - der-stand what love is, _ love _ is, for the first time, _ oh, yeah.
E♭
F
2.
B♭
Gm
E♭
E♭/F
Can this be first time _ Such a
Cm7
Dm7
Cm7
long time a - go I had giv - en up on find - ing the e -
B♭
F/A
Gm7
F/A
Cm7
Dm7
mo - tion _ ev-er a - gain. _ But you're here with me now. Yes, I

Cm7
Cm7/F
found you some - how, and I've nev - er been so

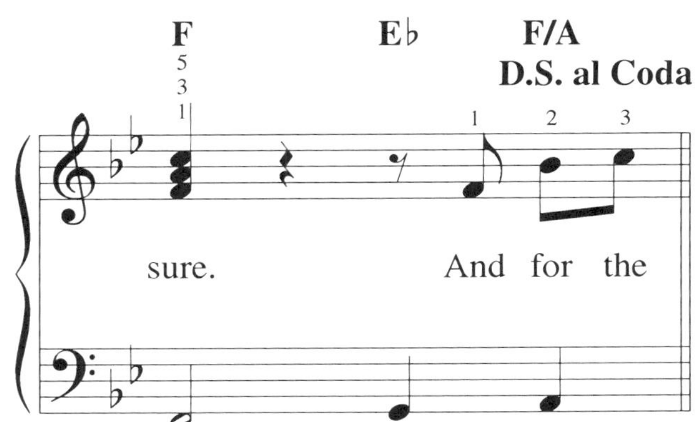
F
E♭
F/A
D.S. al Coda
sure. And for the

CODA
B♭/F
E♭
look-ing back at me.

E♭m
B♭/F
Gm
Cm7
F
Now I'll un - der-stand what love is,
love is, for the

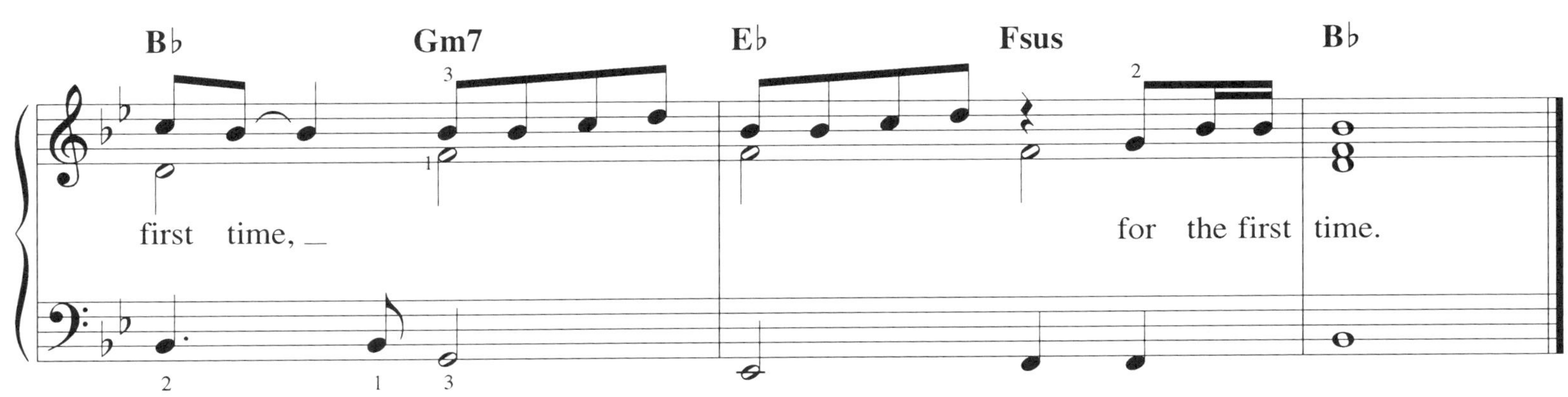
B♭
Gm7
E♭
Fsus
B♭
first time,
for the first time.

GO THE DISTANCE

from Walt Disney Pictures' HERCULES

Music by ALAN MENKEN
Lyrics by DAVID ZIPPEL

C D G C D Em
crowds will cheer when they see my face, and a
thou - sand years would be worth the wait. It might
C B Em G/D C Dsus D
voice keeps say - ing this is where I'm meant to be. I'll be
take a life - time, but some - how I'll see it through. And I
G/B Am/C G/D D D/C
there some - day. I can go the dis - tance. I will
won't look back. I can go the dis - tance. And I'll
G/B Am/C G/D D D/C
find my way if I can be strong. I know
stay on track. No, I won't ac - cept de - feat. It's an

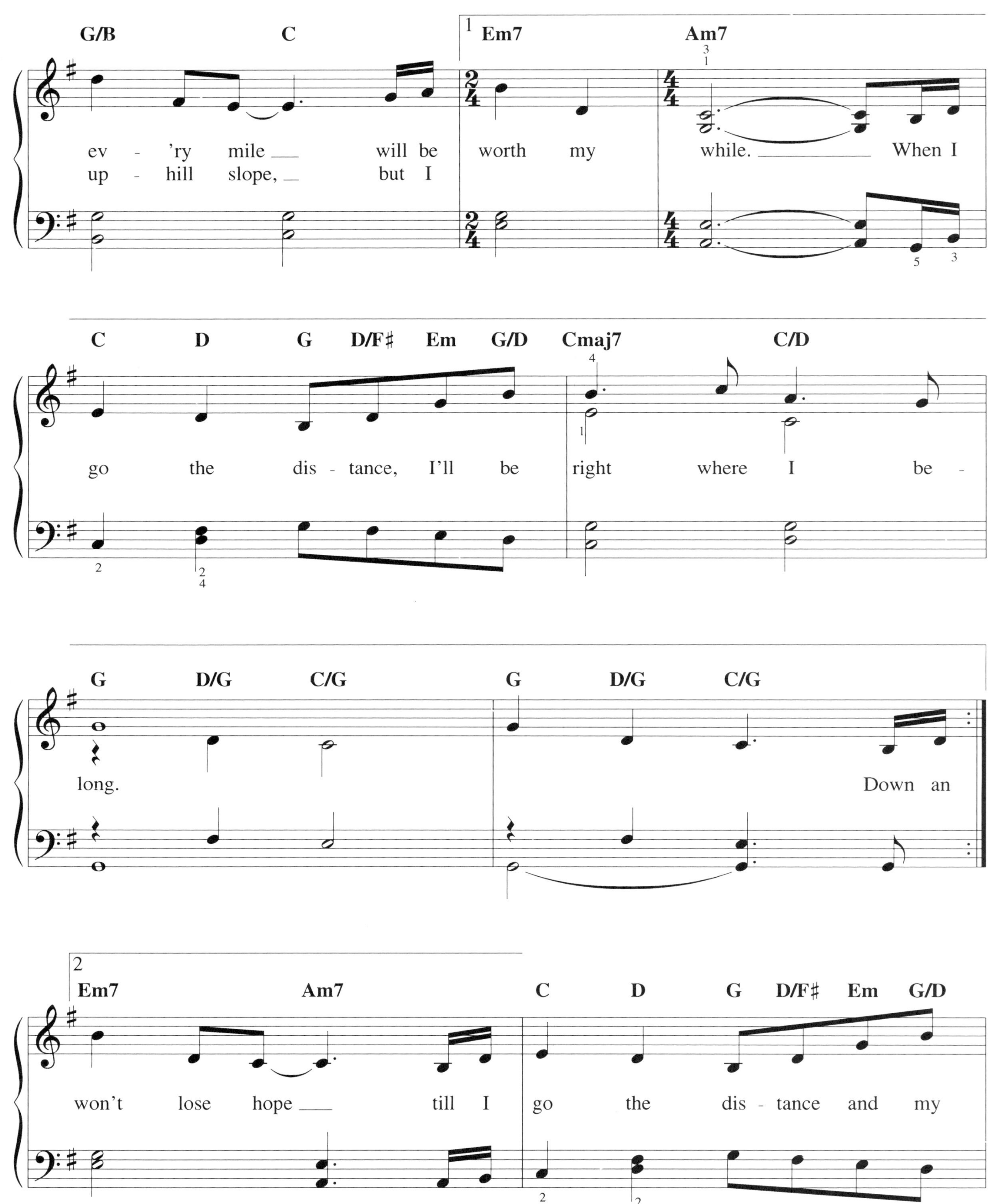
G/B
C
1
Em7
Am7
ev - 'ry mile will be worth my while. When I
up - hill slope, but I
C
D
G
D/F♯
Em
G/D
Cmaj7
C/D
go the dis - tance, I'll be right where I be -
G
D/G
C/G
long. Down an
2
won't lose hope till I go the dis - tance and my

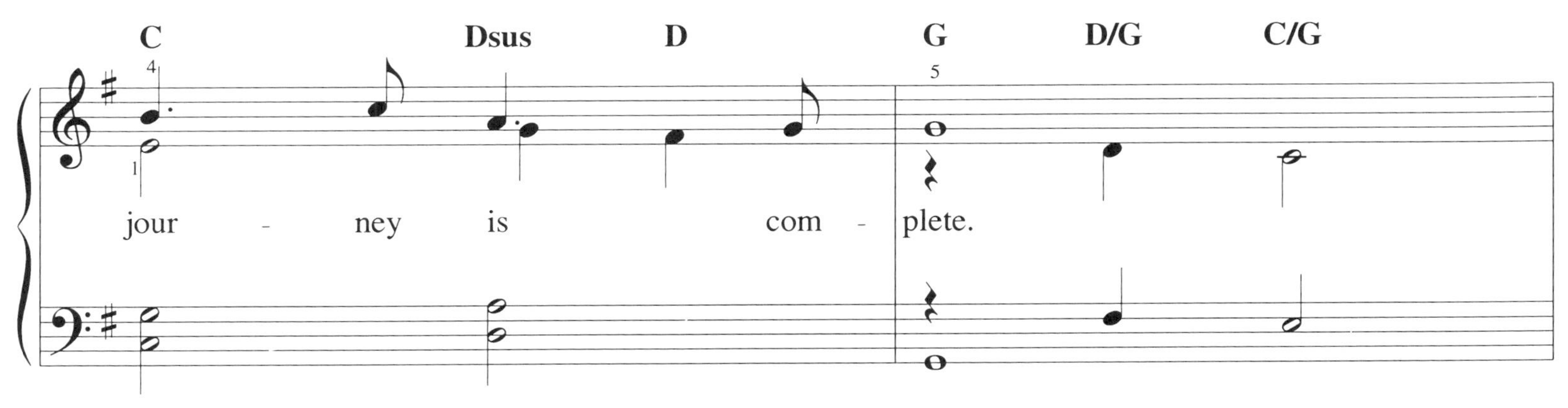
C
Dsus
D
G
D/G
C/G
jour - ney is com - plete.

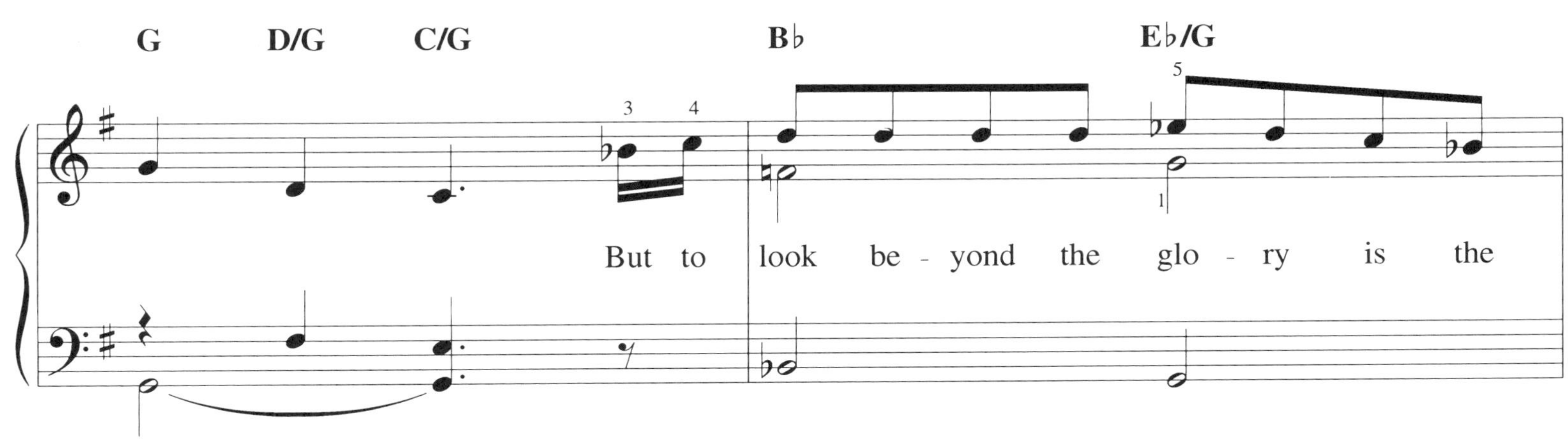
G
D/G
C/G
B♭
E♭/G
But to look be - yond the glo - ry is the

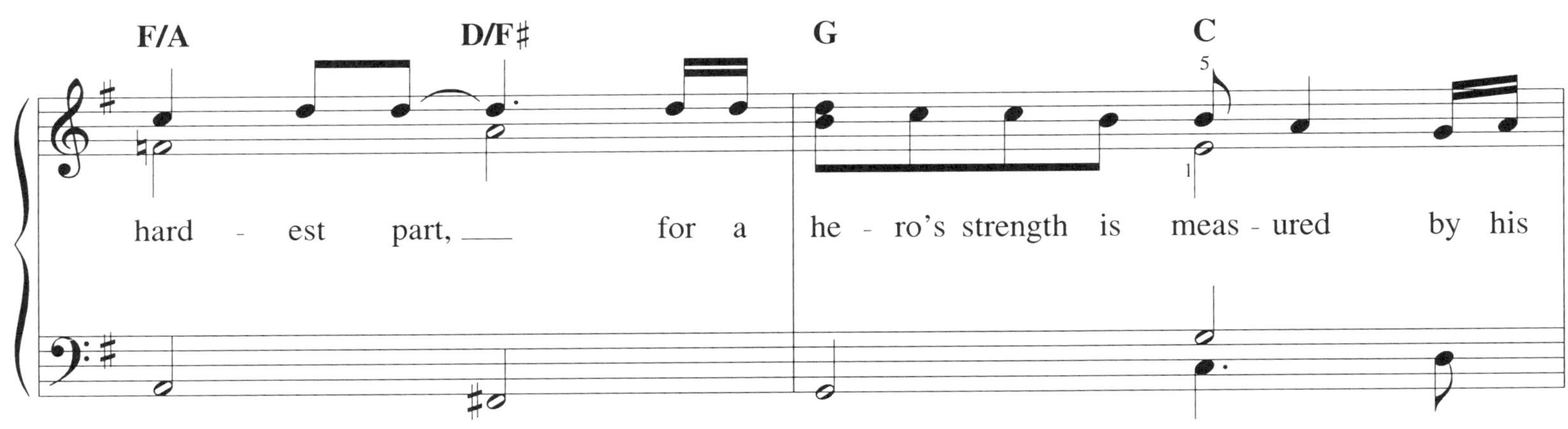
F/A
D/F♯
G
C
hard - est part, for a he - ro's strength is meas - ured by his

B/D♯
G/B
Am/C
heart. Like a shoot - ing star,

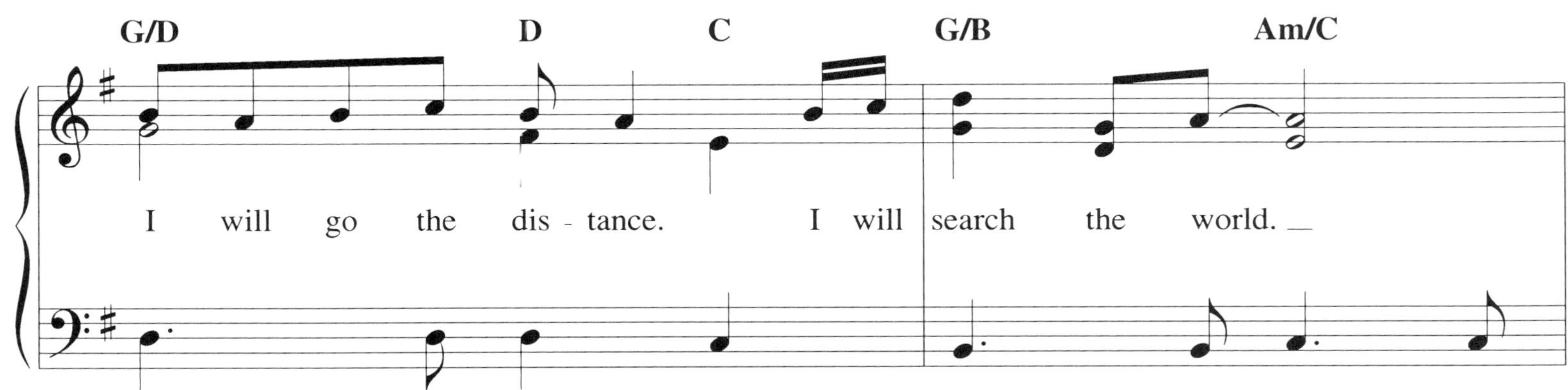
G/D
D
C
G/B
Am/C
I will go the dis - tance. I will search the world.

G/D
D
C
G/B
A/C♯
I will face it's harms. I don't care how far.

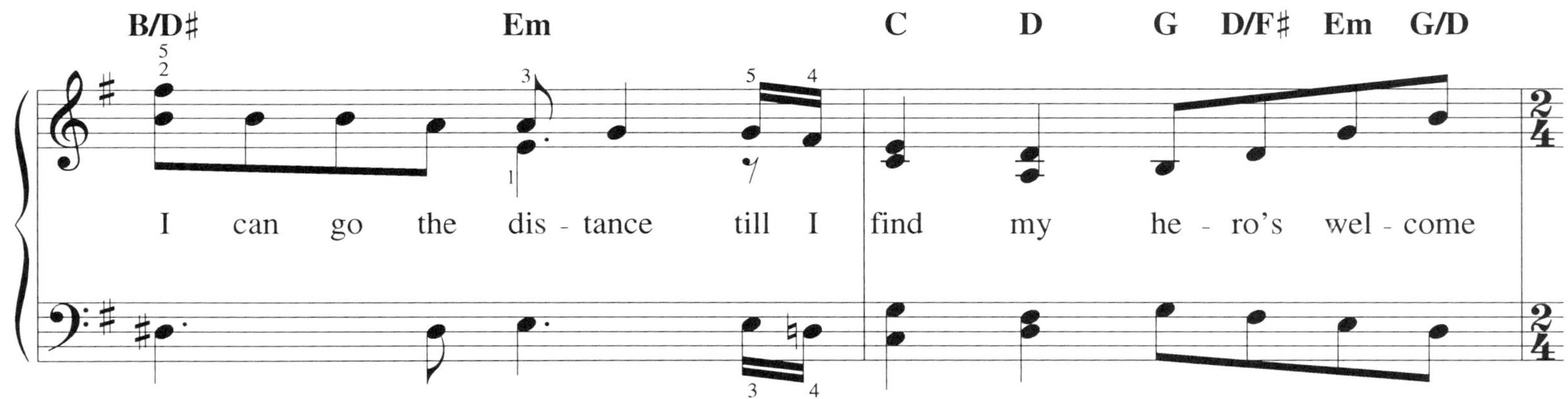
B/D♯
Em
C
D
G
D/F♯
Em
G/D
I can go the dis - tance till I find my he - ro's wel - come

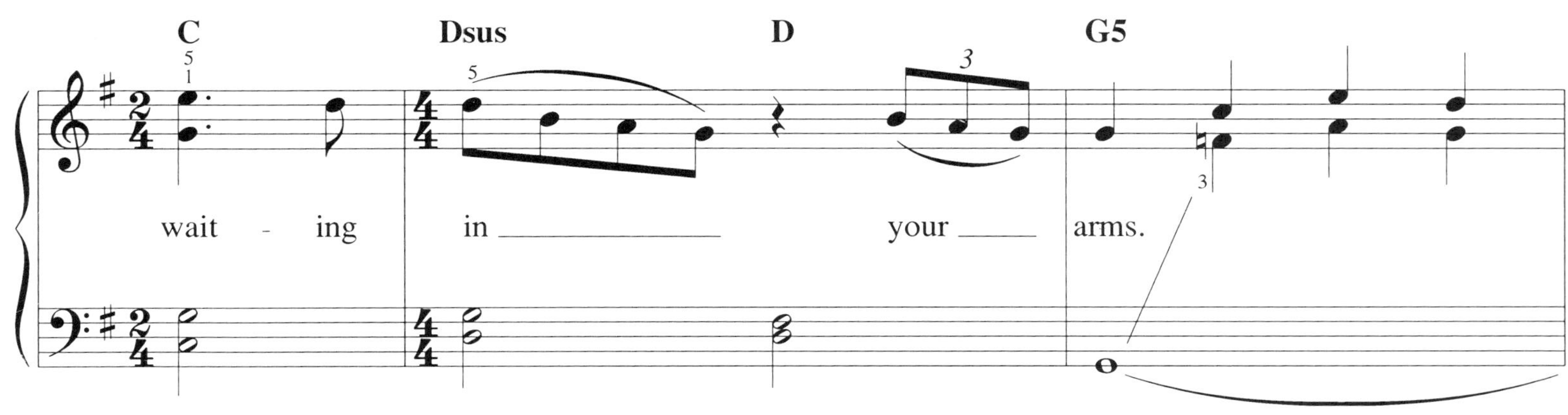
C
Dsus
D
G5
wait - ing in your arms.

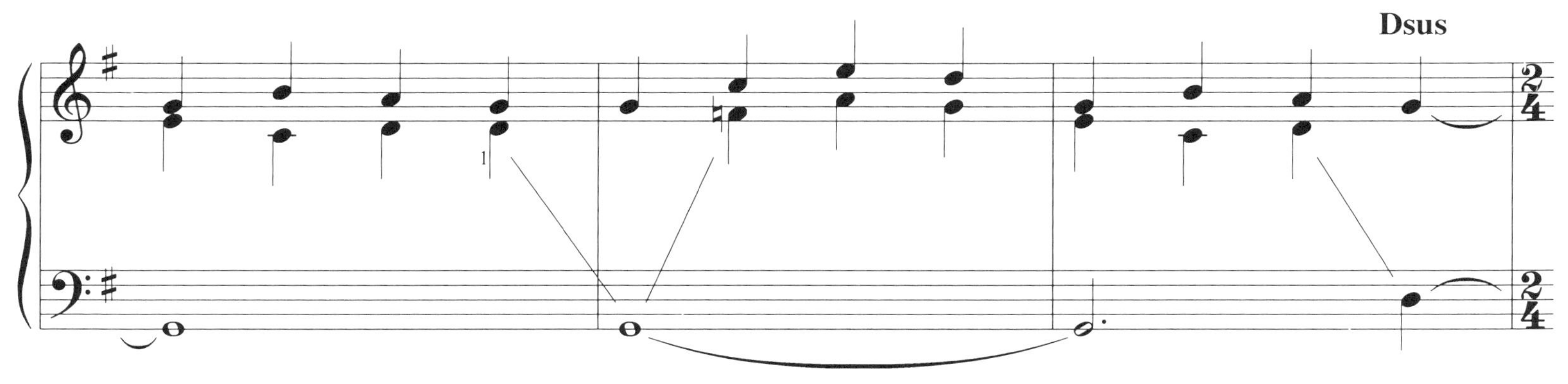
Dsus

G/B
Cmaj7
Em7
I will search the world. I will face it's harms

Am7
C
D
G
D/F♯
Em
G/D
till I find my he - ro's wel - come

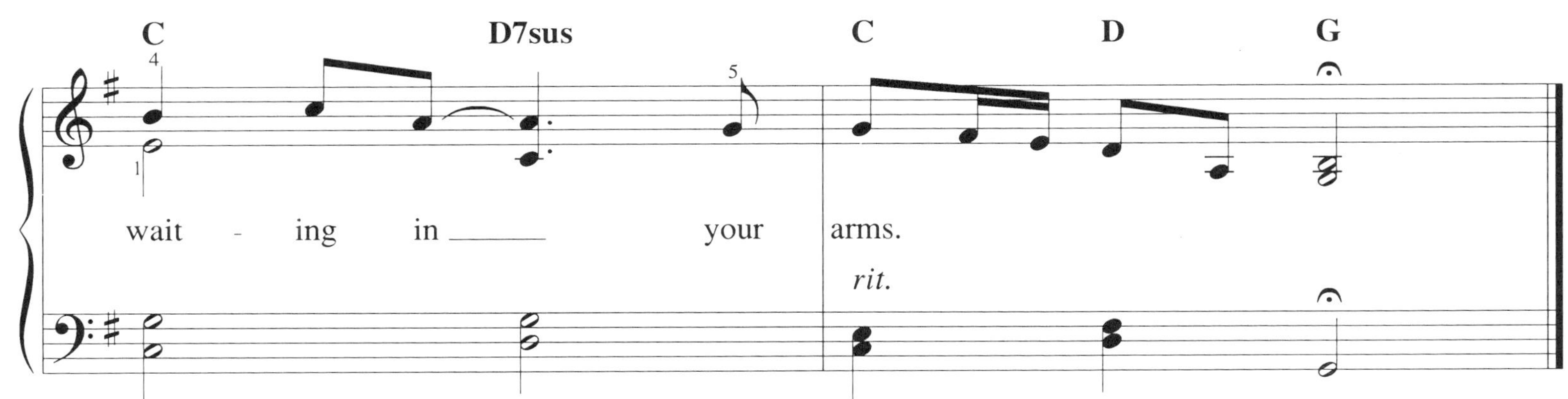
C
D7sus
C
D
G
wait - ing in your arms.
rit.

I FINALLY FOUND SOMEONE

from THE MIRROR HAS TWO FACES

Words and Music by BARBRA STREISAND, MARVIN HAMLISCH,
R.J. LANGE and BRYAN ADAMS

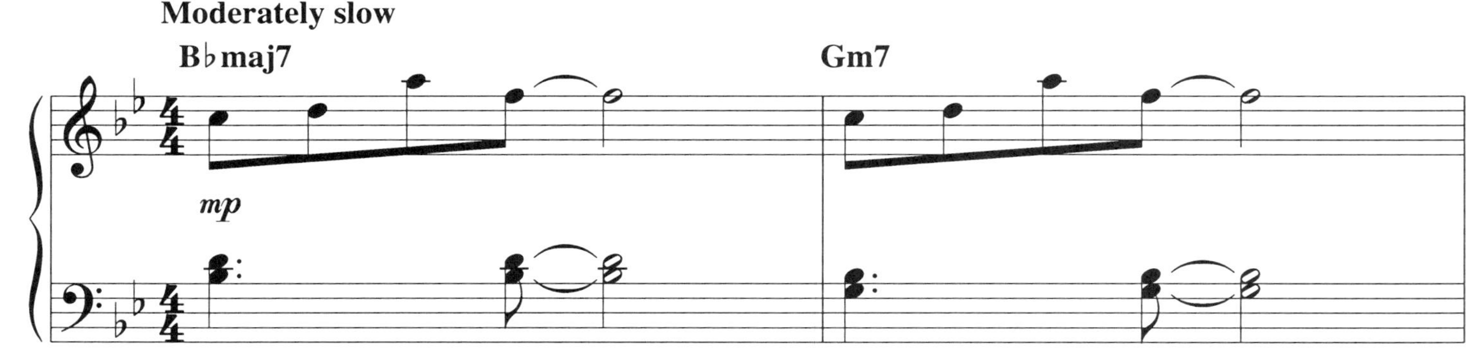

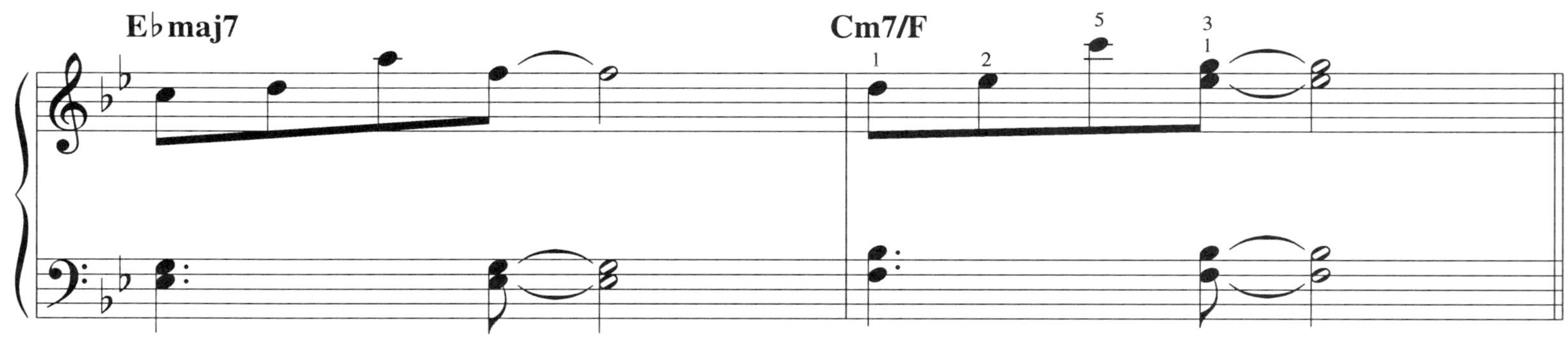

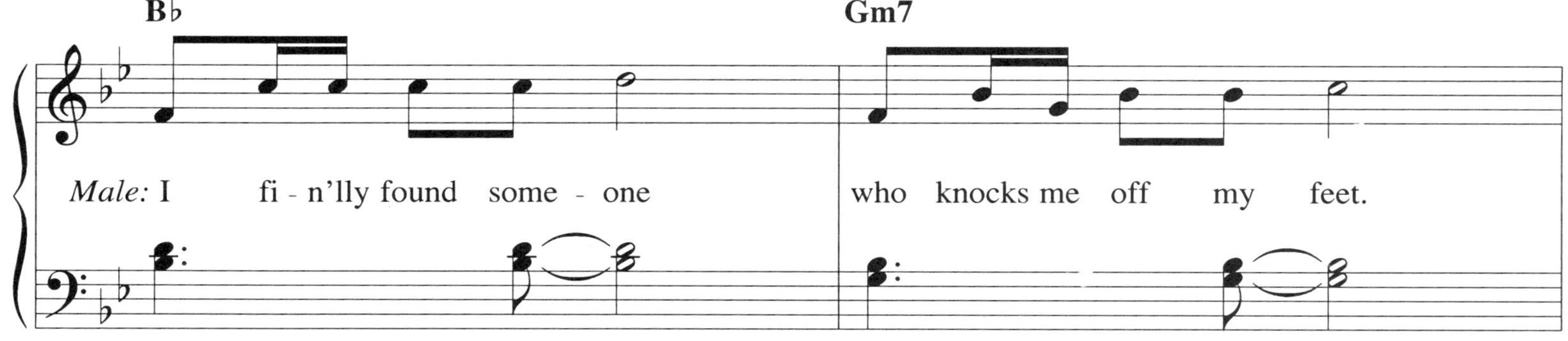

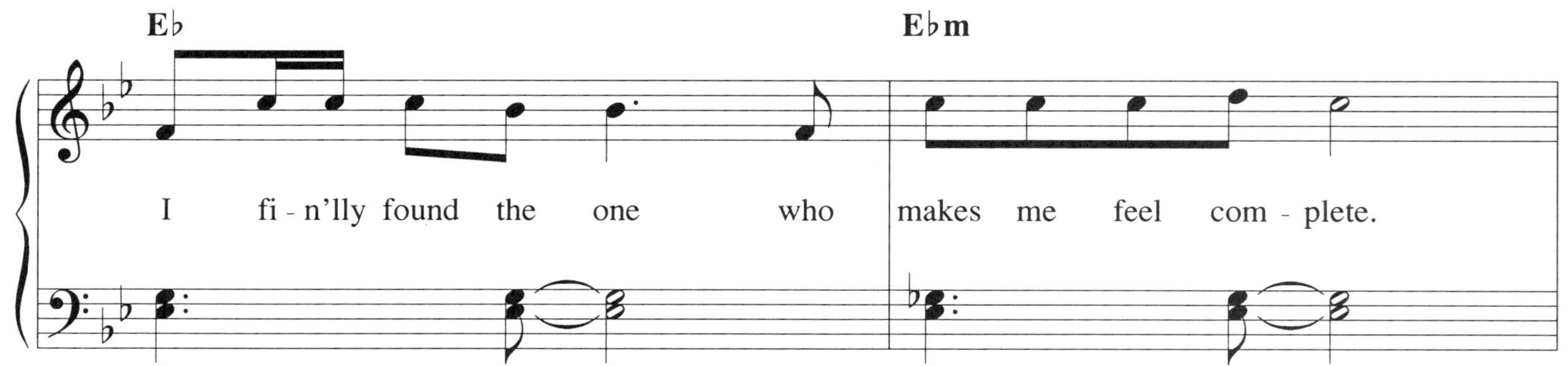

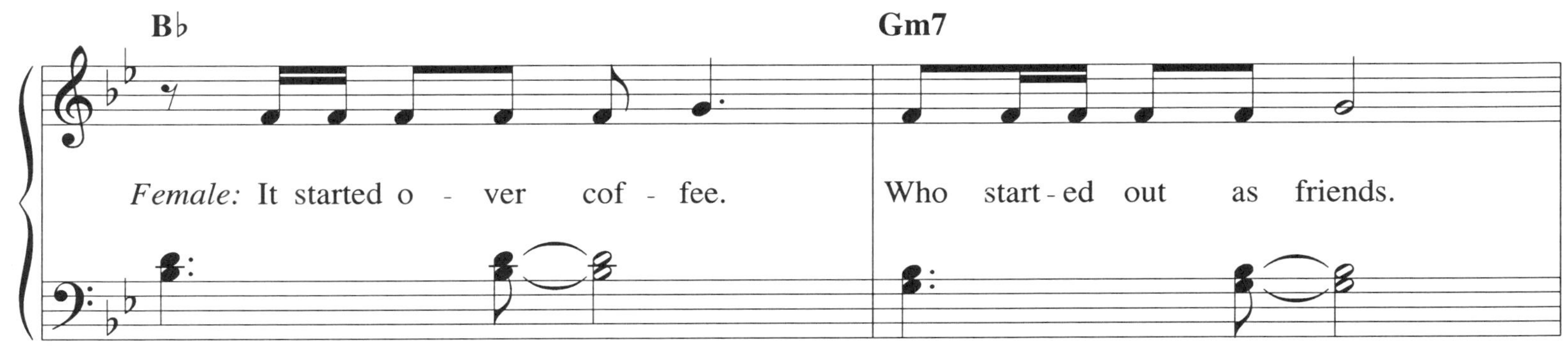
B♭
Gm7
Female: It started o - ver cof - fee.
Who start - ed out as friends.

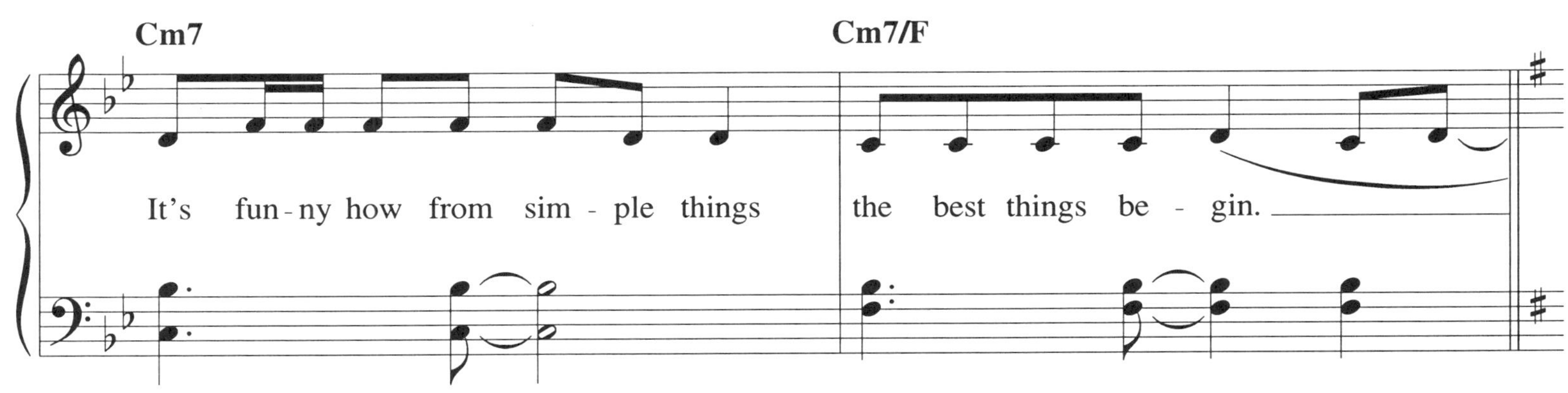
Cm7
Cm7/F
It's fun - ny how from sim - ple things
the best things be - gin.

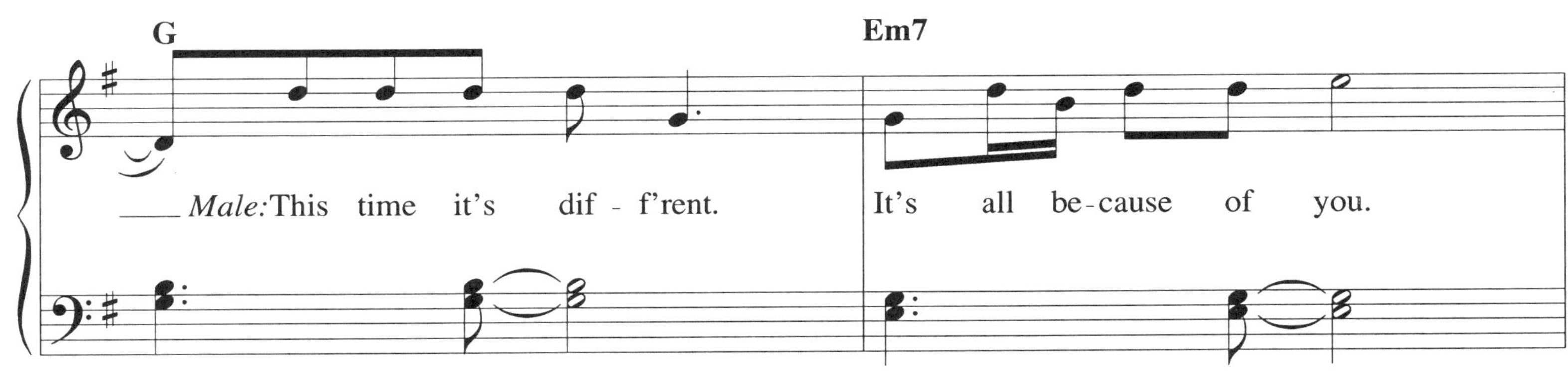
G
Em7
Male: This time it's dif - f'rent.
It's all be - cause of you.

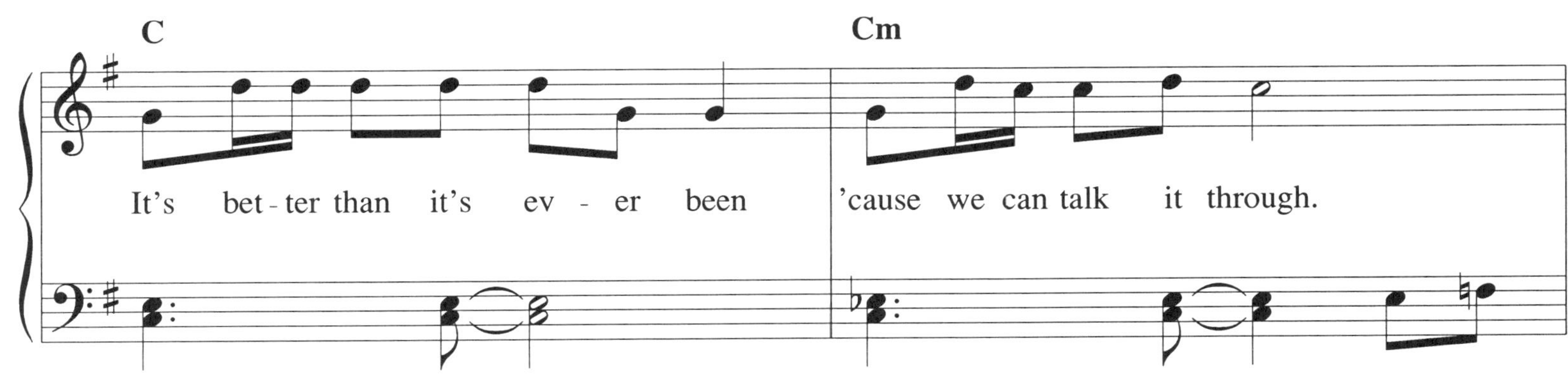
C
Cm
It's bet - ter than it's ev - er been
'cause we can talk it through.

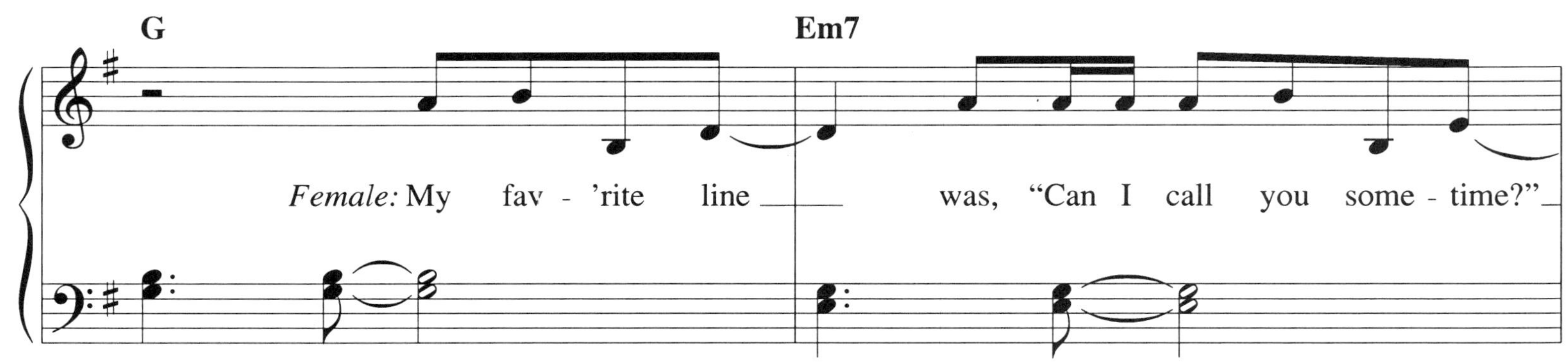
G
Em7
Female: My fav - 'rite line
was, "Can I call you some - time?"

Cmaj7
Cm
It's all you had to say to
take my breath a - way.

E
Amaj7
Am6
mf
Both: This is it. Oh, I fi - n'lly
found some - one, some -

E
Amaj7
Am6
one to share my life. I fi - n'lly
found the one to

E
G♯sus
G♯
be with ev - 'ry night. Female: 'Cause what - ev - er I do, ___ Male: it's just

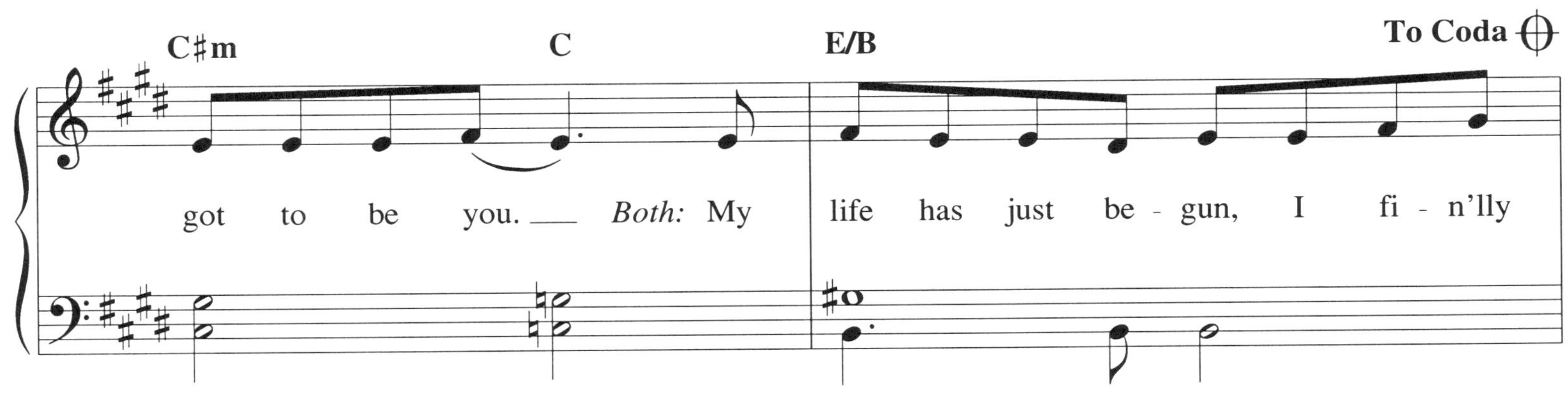
C♯m
C
E/B
To Coda
got to be you. ___ Both: My life has just be - gun, I fi - n'lly

F♯m/B
E
found some - one.
mp

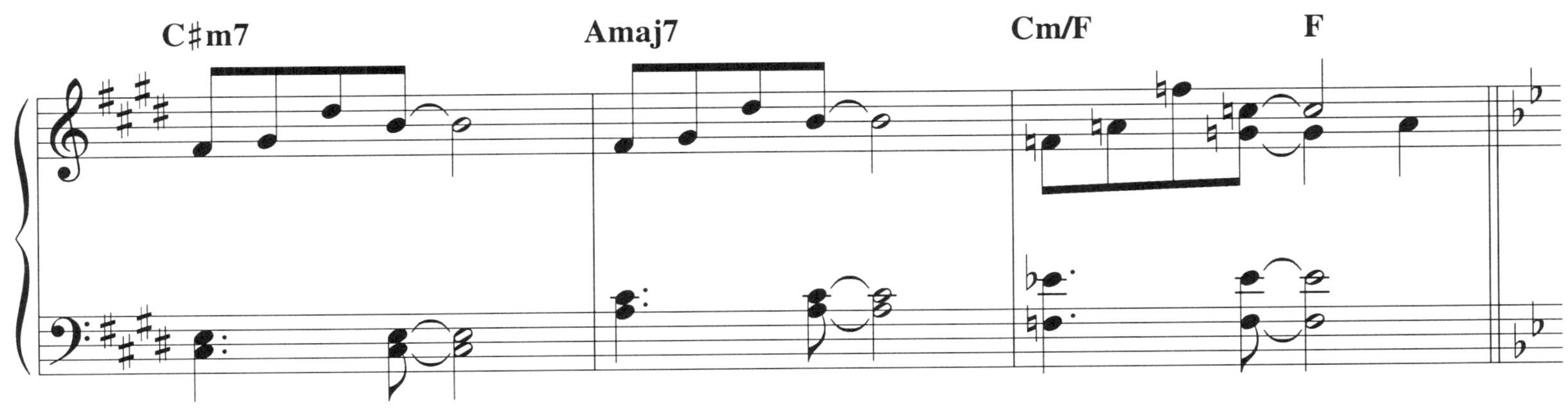
C♯m7
Amaj7
Cm/F
F

B♭
Gm
Male: Did I keep you wait - ing?
I a - pol - o - gize.
mf
Female: I didn't mind.
Baby, that's fine.

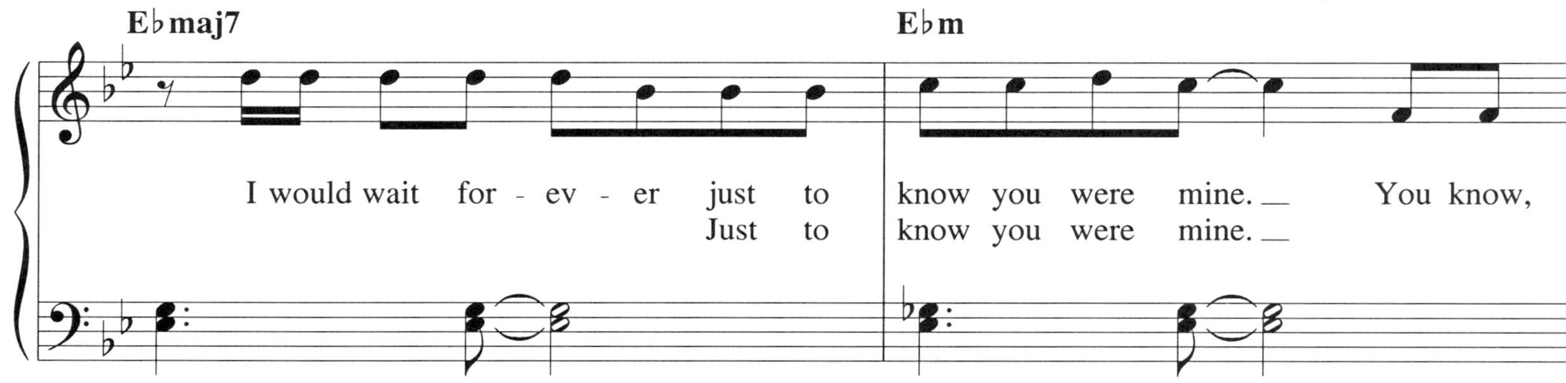
E♭maj7
E♭m
I would wait for - ev - er just to
know you were mine.
You know,
Just to
know you were mine.

B♭
Gm
I love your hair.
I
love what you wear.
Are you sure it looks right?
Isn't it too tight?

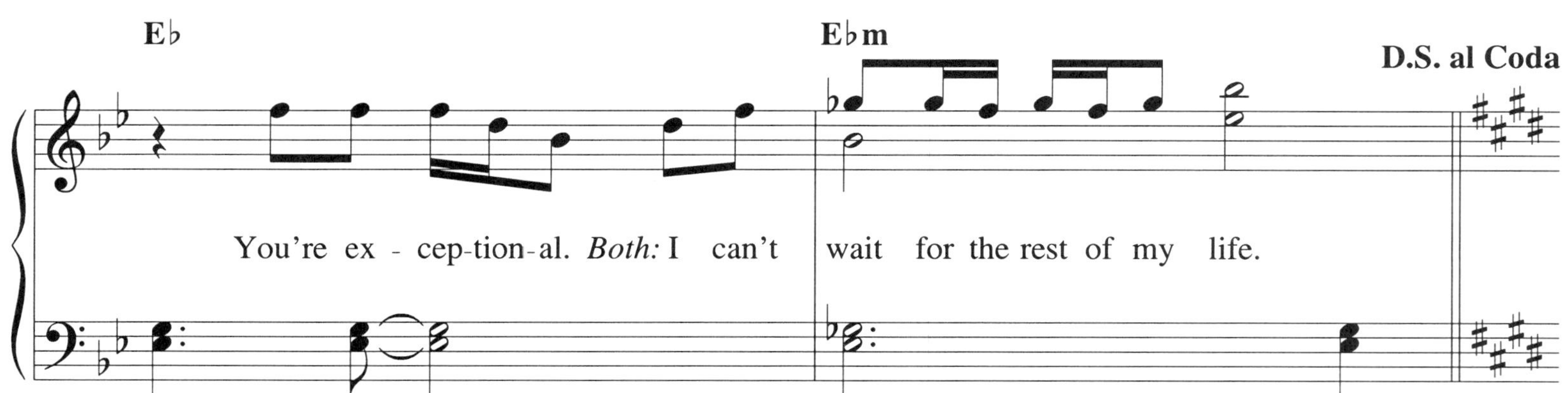
E♭
E♭m
D.S. al Coda
You're ex - cep-tion-al. Both: I can't
wait for the rest of my life.

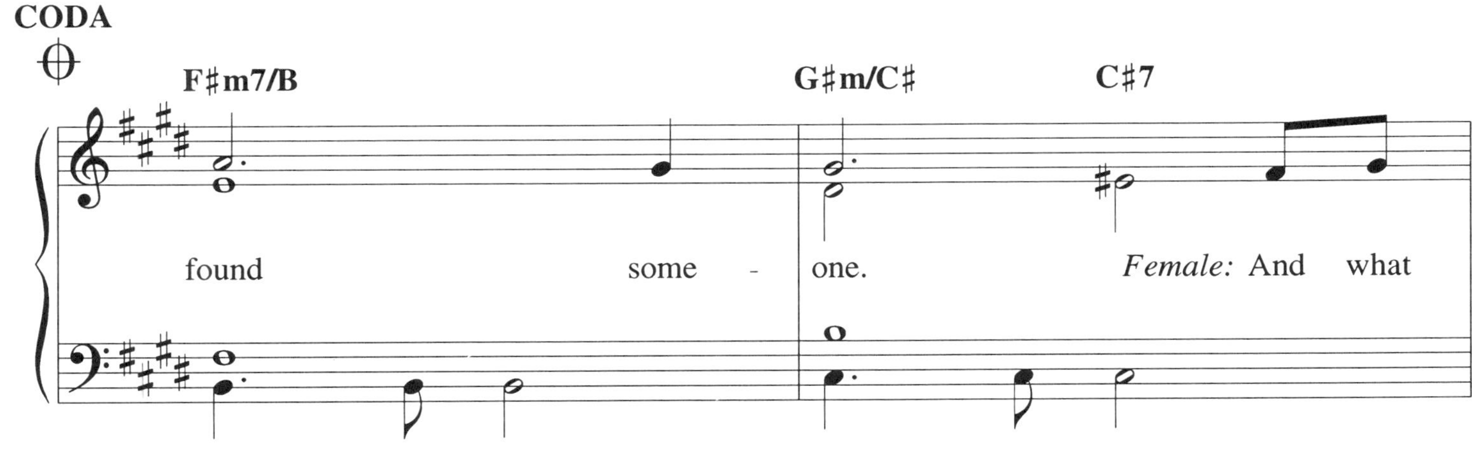
CODA
F♯m7/B
G♯m/C♯
C♯7
found some - one. Female: And what

F♯m7
E/G♯
ev - er I do, Male: it's just got to be you. Female: My

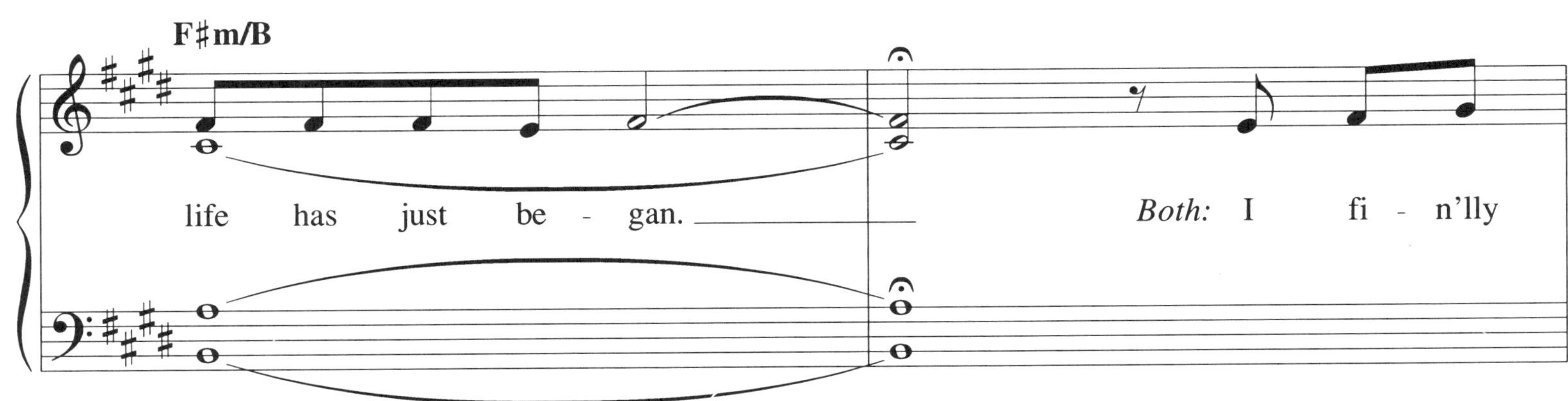
F♯m/B
life has just be - gan. Both: I fi - n'lly

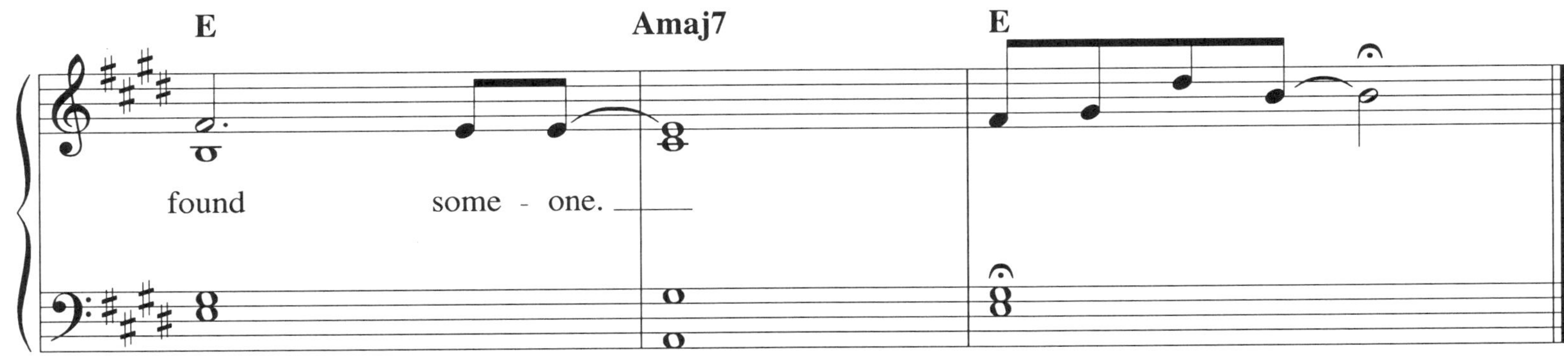
E
Amaj7
E
found some - one.

IF WE FALL IN LOVE TONIGHT

Words and Music by JAMES HARRIS III
and TERRY LEWIS

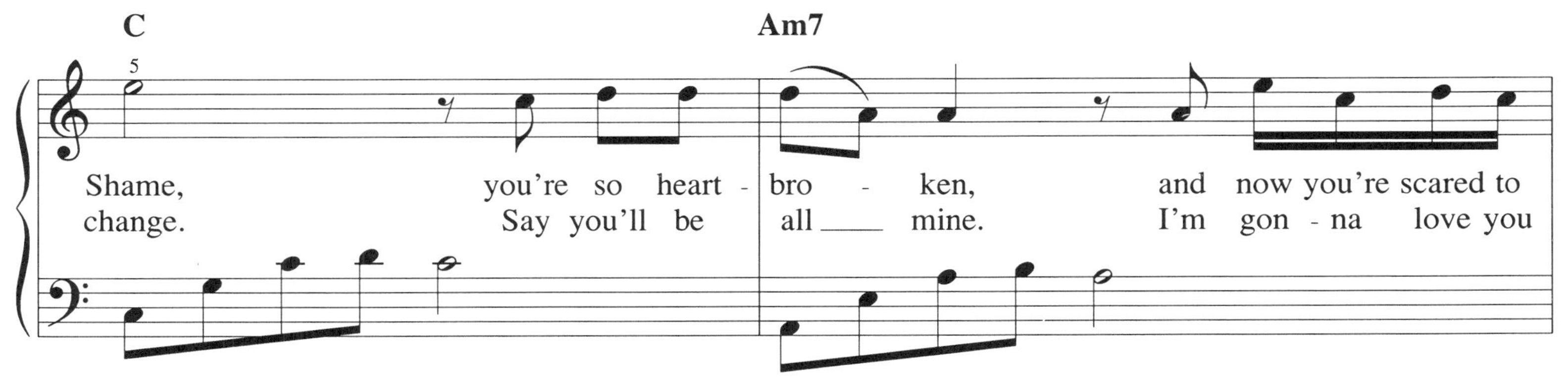
C
Am7
Shame, you're so heart - bro - ken, and now you're scared to
change. Say you'll be all ___ mine. I'm gon - na love you

Fmaj7
G6
o - pen and give your love a - gain.
all the time. Don't let it slip a - way.
And

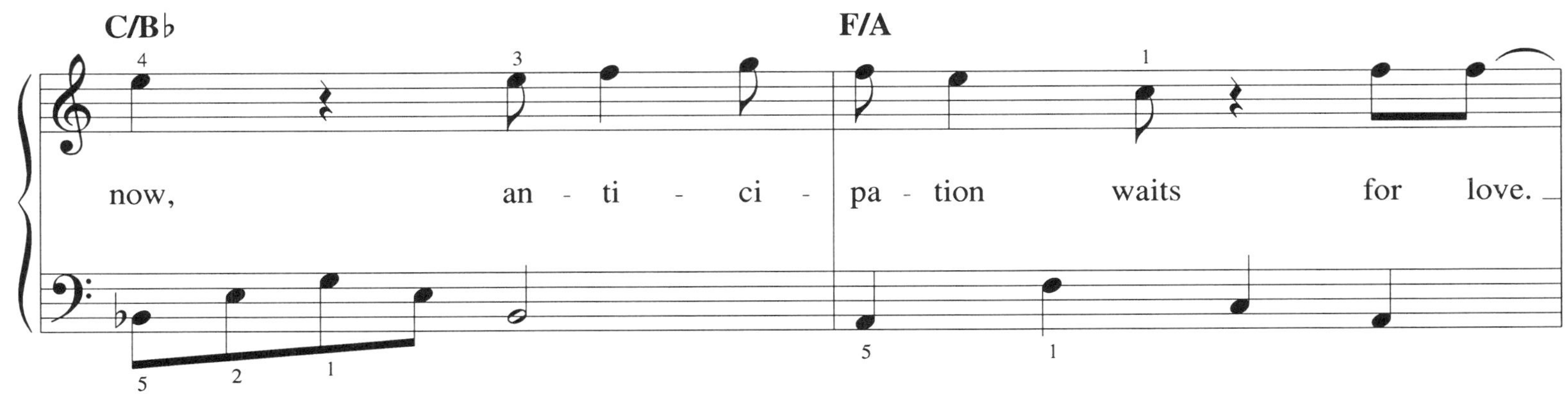
C/B♭
F/A
now, an - ti - ci - pa - tion waits for love.

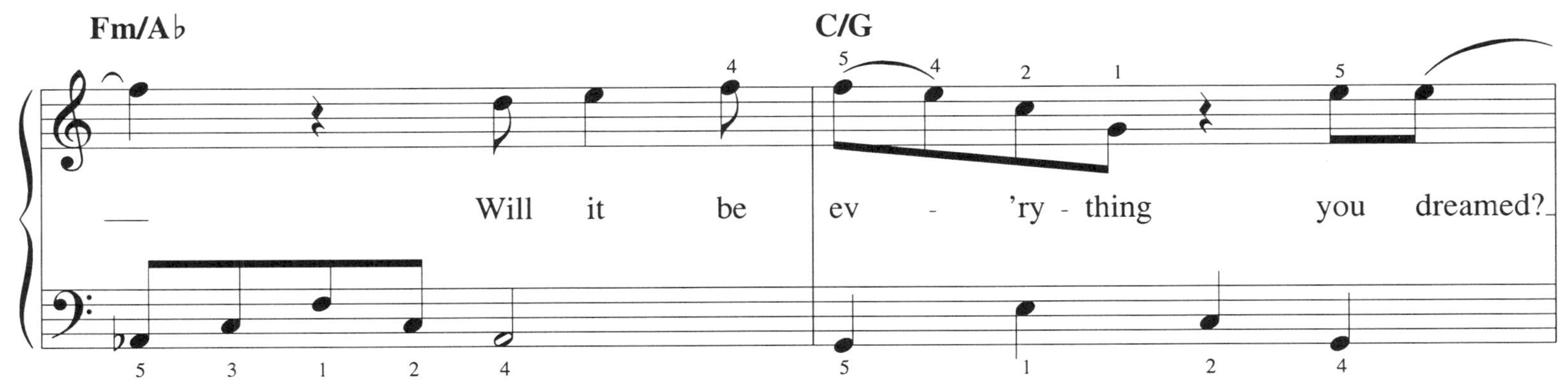
Fm/A♭
C/G
Will it be ev - 'ry - thing you dreamed?

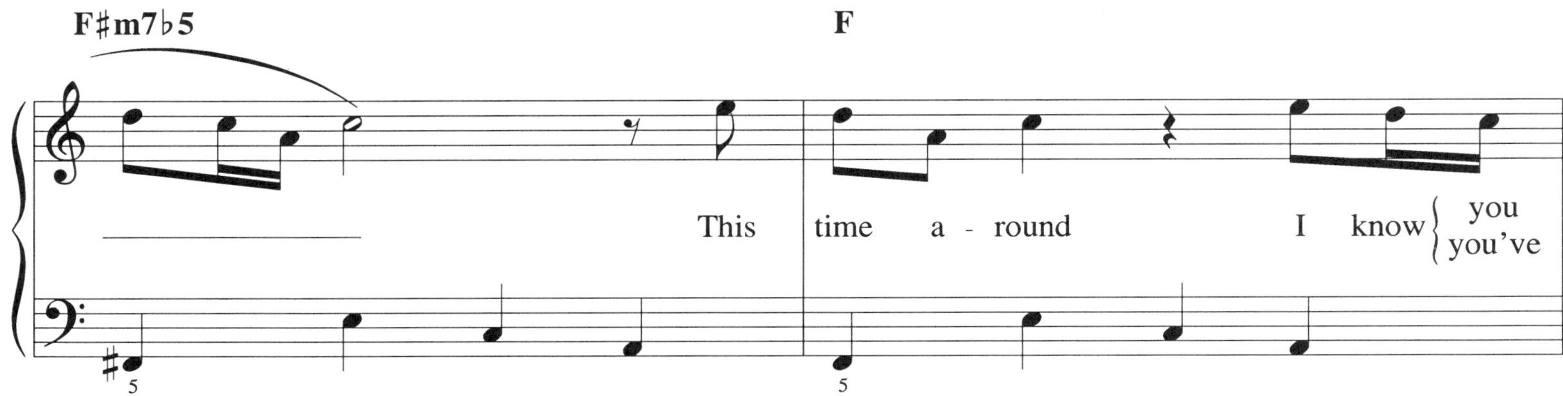
F♯m7♭5
F
This time a - round I know you
you've

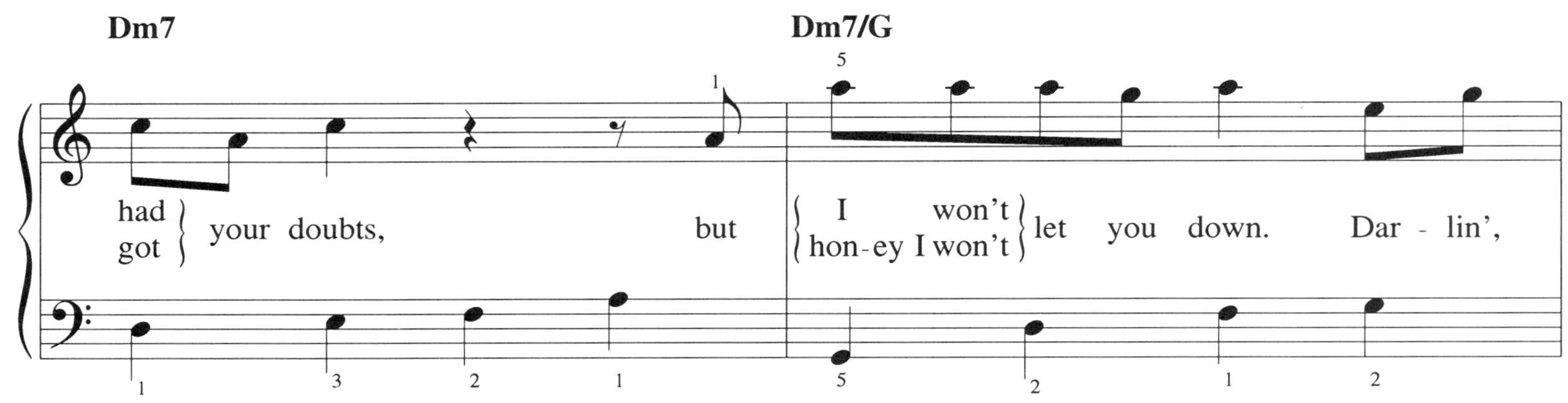
Dm7
Dm7/G
had
got your doubts, but
I won't
hon-ey I won't let you down. Dar - lin',

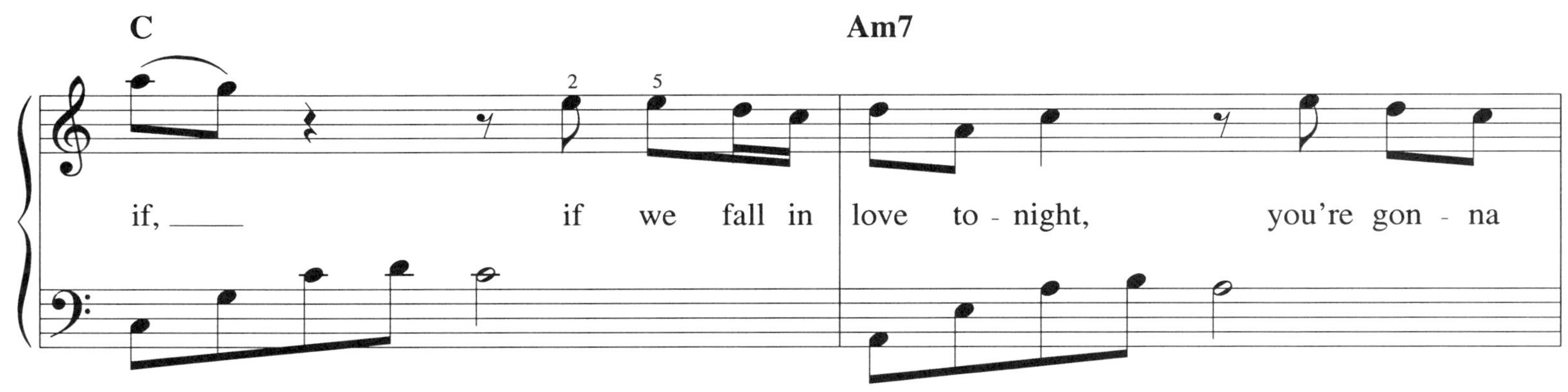
C
Am7
if, if we fall in love to - night, you're gon - na

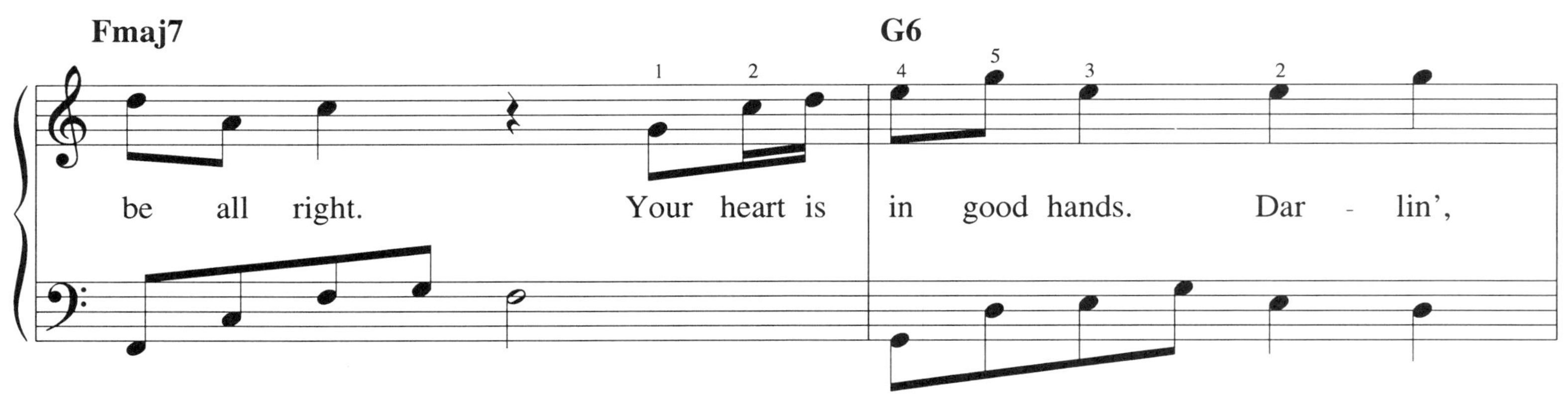
Fmaj7
G6
be all right. Your heart is in good hands. Dar - lin',

C
Am7
if, ___ if we fall in love a - gain, on me you

Fmaj7
G6
can de - pend if you can take a chance.

C
Am
F
O - pen your heart and let love love a -

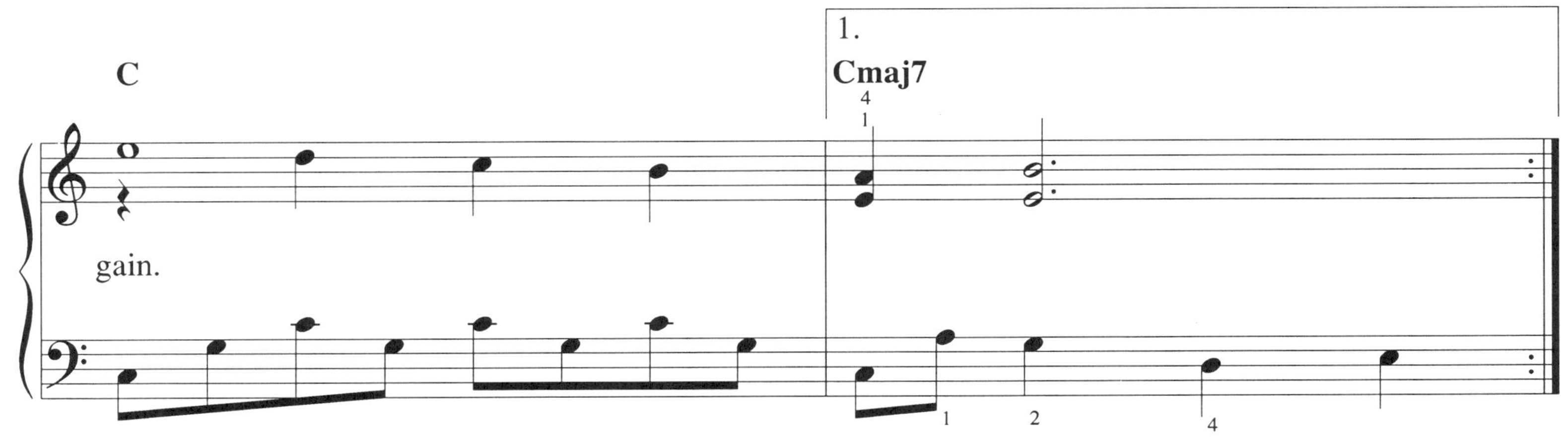
C
1.
Cmaj7
gain.

2.
Cmaj7
Dm7
Em7
Fmaj7
3
3
Hon - ey I
don't I don't want you to

Em7
Am7
Dm7
Dm7/G
have an - y doubts _ a - bout
me. What - ev - er makes you hap - py,

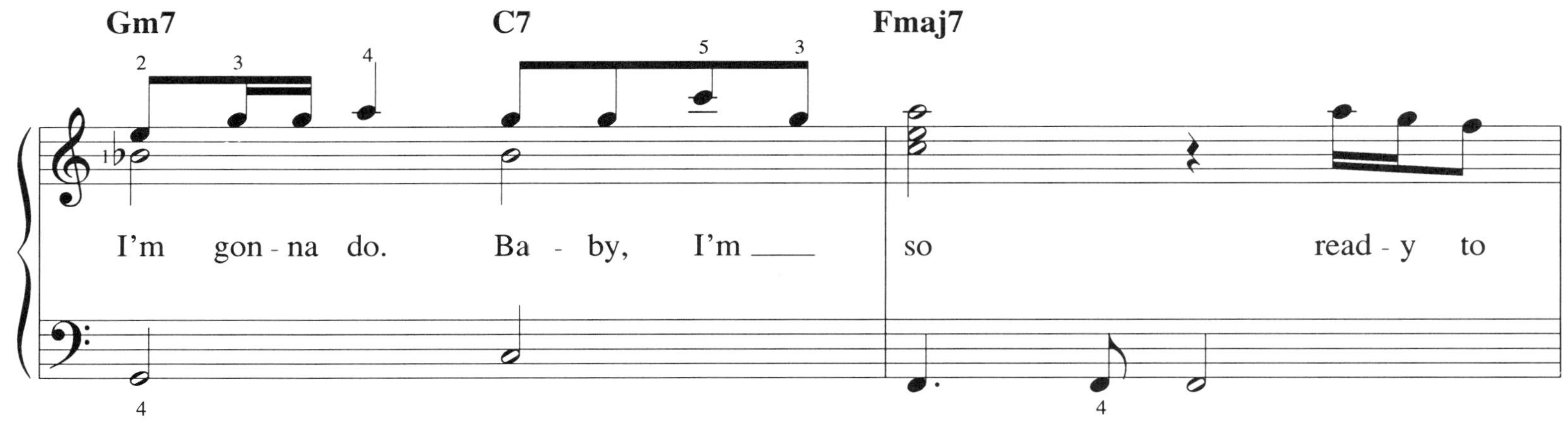
Gm7
C7
Fmaj7
I'm gon - na do. Ba - by, I'm ___
so read - y to

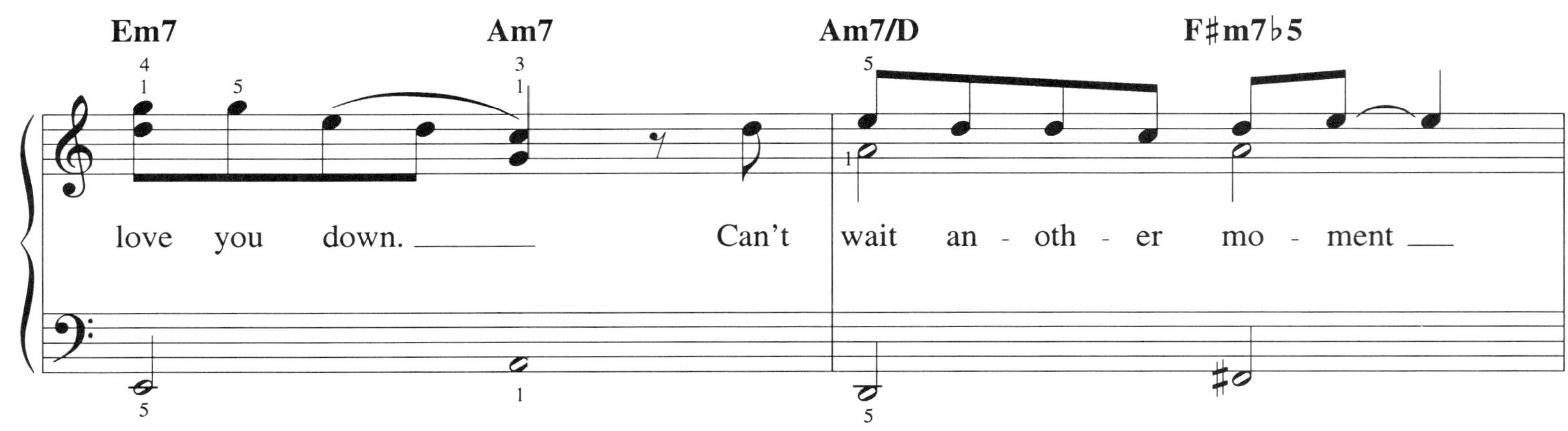
Em7
Am7
Am7/D
F♯m7♭5
love you down. ______ Can't
wait an - oth - er mo - ment __

Dm7/G
B7/A
D
Bm7
be here right now. Dar-lin',
if, __
if we fall in
love to-night,
you're gon-na

Gmaj7
A6
D
be all right.
Your heart is
in good hands. Dar - lin',
if, __
if we fall in

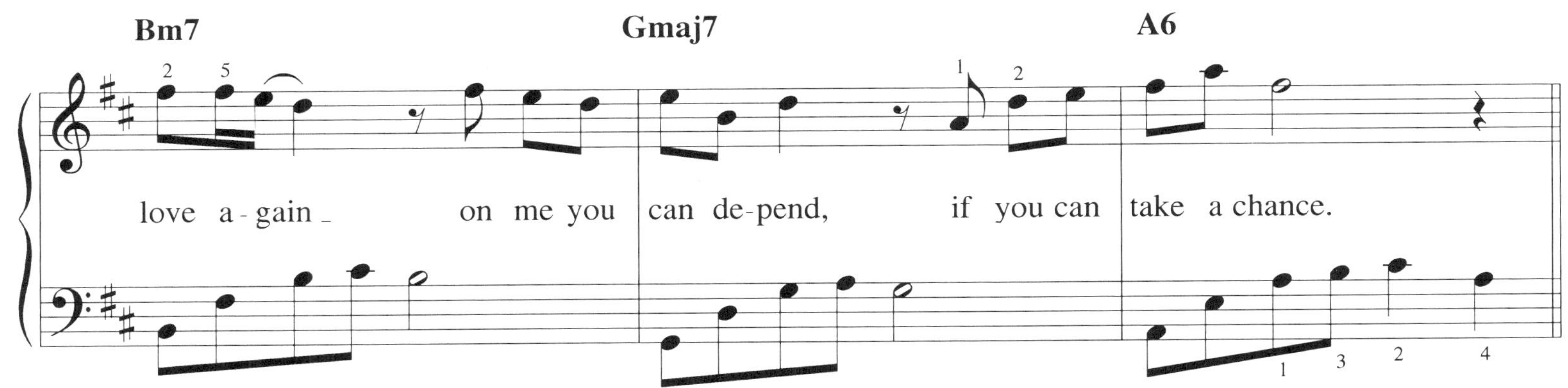
Bm7
Gmaj7
A6
love a - gain _
on me you
can de-pend,
if you can
take a chance.

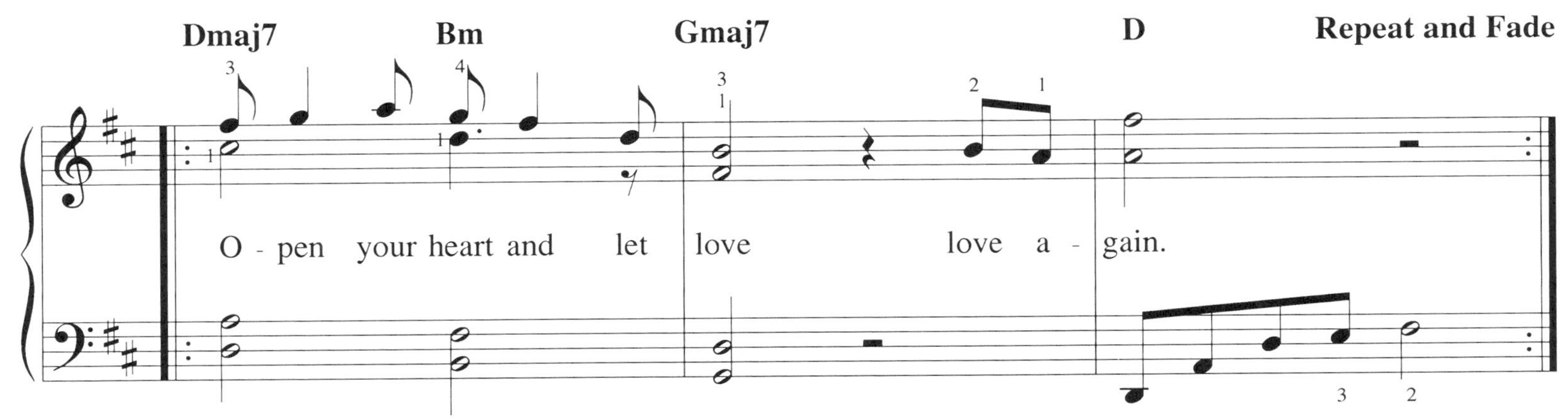
Dmaj7
Bm
Gmaj7
D
Repeat and Fade
O - pen your heart and let
love
love a -
gain.

IT'S ALL COMING BACK TO ME NOW

Words and Music by
JIM STEINMAN

F C/G G Em Am
ev - er.
I fin - ished cry - ing in the
Thought you were his - t'ry with the
F G7 C Em Am F Gsus G
in - stant that you left, and I can't re - mem - ber where or when or how. And I
slam - ming of the door, and I made my - self so strong a - gain some - how. And I
Em Am F G F
ban - ished ev - 'ry mem - 'ry you and I had ev - er made.
nev - er was - ted an - y of my time on you since then.
rit.
F/G C G/B
But when you touch me like this, and you hold me like that, I just
But if I touch you like this, and if you kiss me like that, it was
a tempo

Am Dm F G7
have to ad - mit that it's all com - ing back to me. When I
so long a - go but it's all com - ing back to me. If you

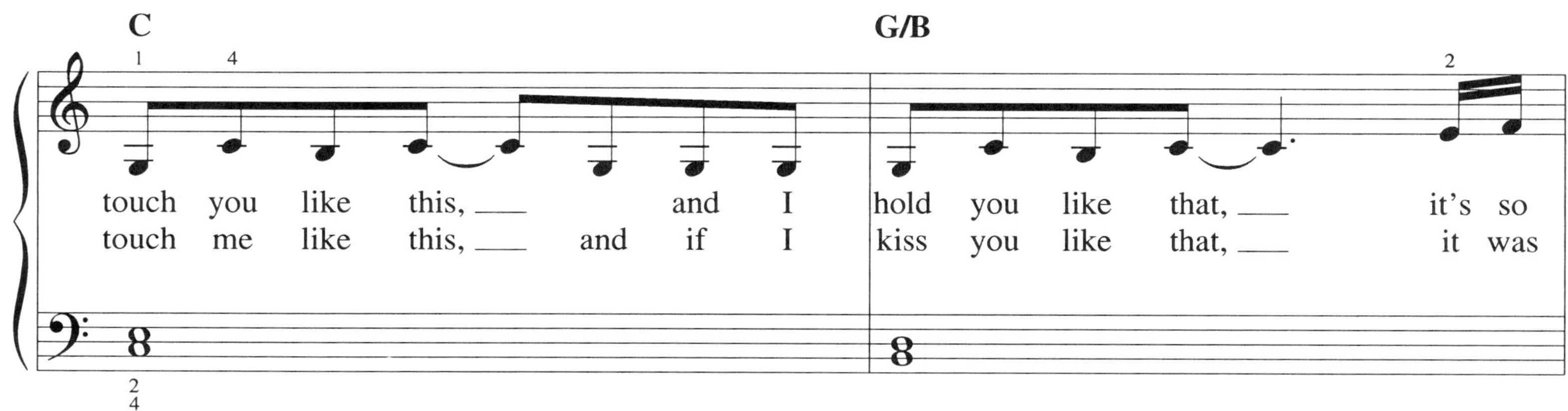
C G/B
touch you like this, and I hold you like that, it's so
touch me like this, and if I kiss you like that, it was

Am7 Dm F G7
hard to be - lieve, but it's all com - ing back to me.
gone with the wind, but it's all com - ing back to me.
It's

C F G
all com - ing back, it's all com - ing back to me now. There were

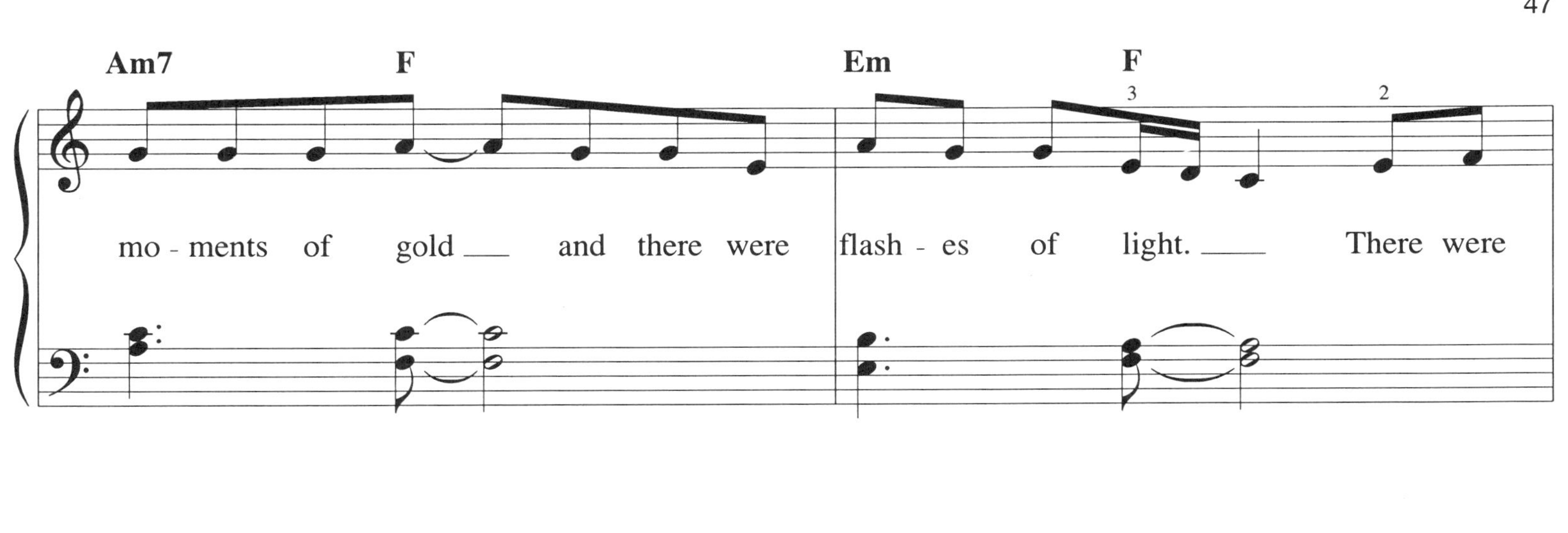
Am7
F
Em
F
mo - ments of gold ___ and there were
flash - es of light. ___ There were

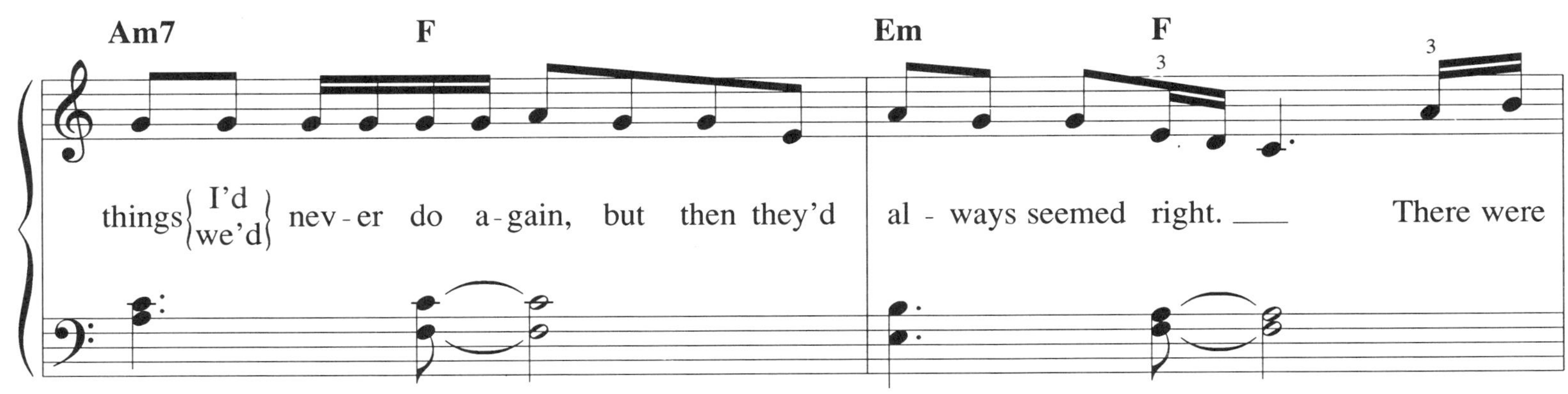
Am7
F
Em
F
things {I'd / we'd} nev - er do a - gain, but then they'd
al - ways seemed right. ___ There were

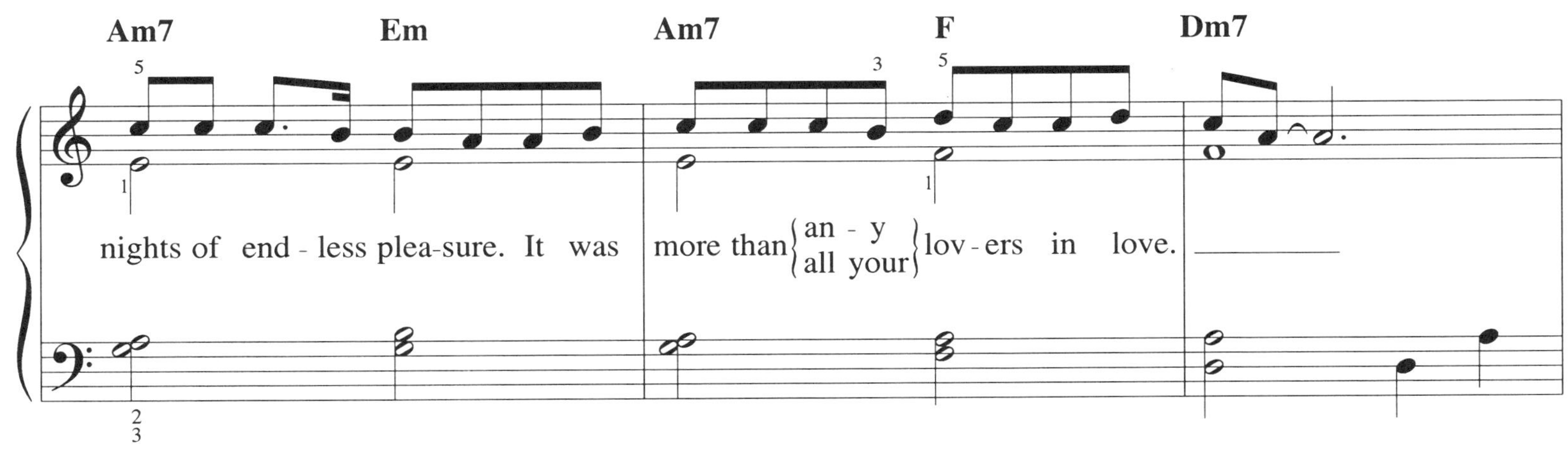
Am7
Em
Am7
F
Dm7
nights of end - less plea-sure. It was
more than {an - y / all your} lov - ers in love. ___

F/G
C
G/B
Ba - by, ba - by, if I
kiss you like this, _ and if you
whis - per like that, _ it was
Ba - by, ba - by, when you
touch me like this, _ and when you
hold me like that, _ it was

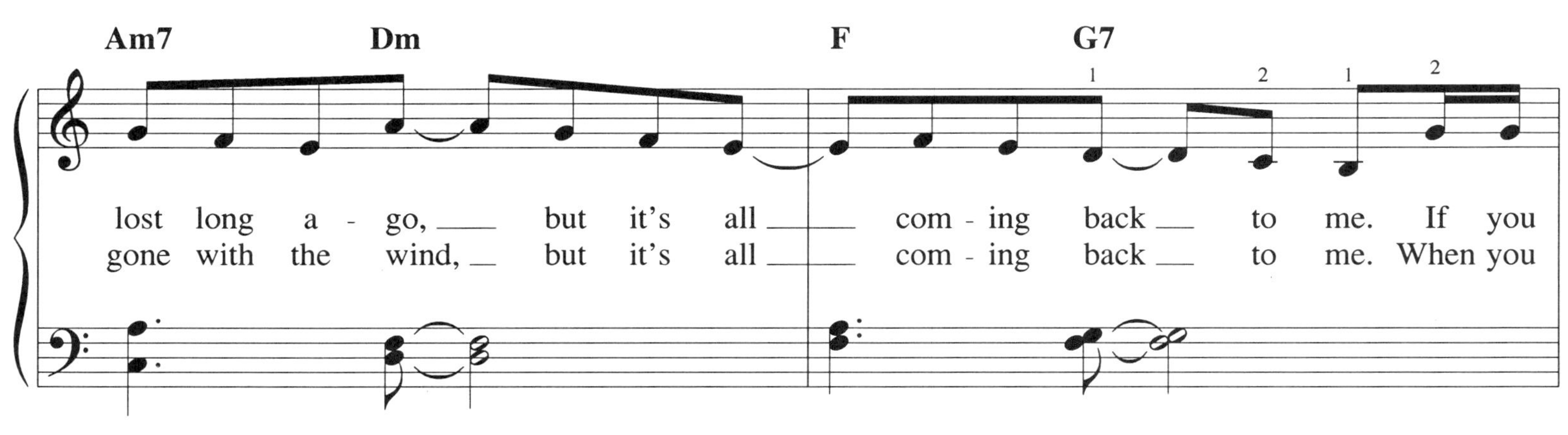
Am7 Dm F G7
lost long a - go, but it's all com - ing back to me. If you
gone with the wind, but it's all com - ing back to me. When you

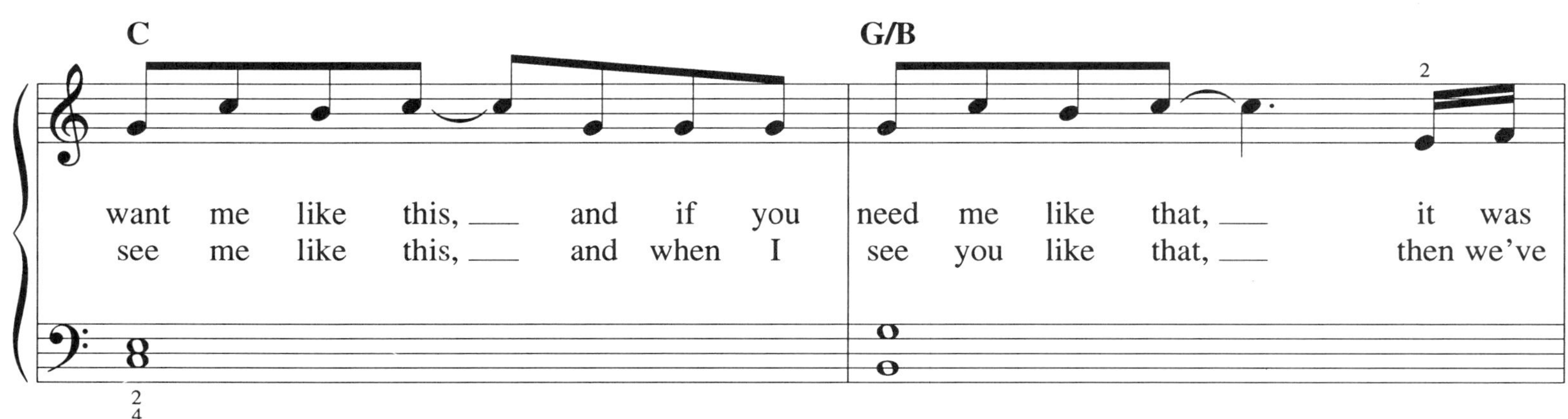
C G/B
want me like this, and if you need me like that, it was
see me like this, and when I see you like that, then we've

Am7 Dm F G7
that long a - go, but it's all com - ing back to me. It's so
seen what we want, to see all com - ing back to me. The

Am7 Dm F G7
hard to re - sist, and it's all com - ing back to me.
flesh and the fan - ta - sies all com - ing back to me.
I can

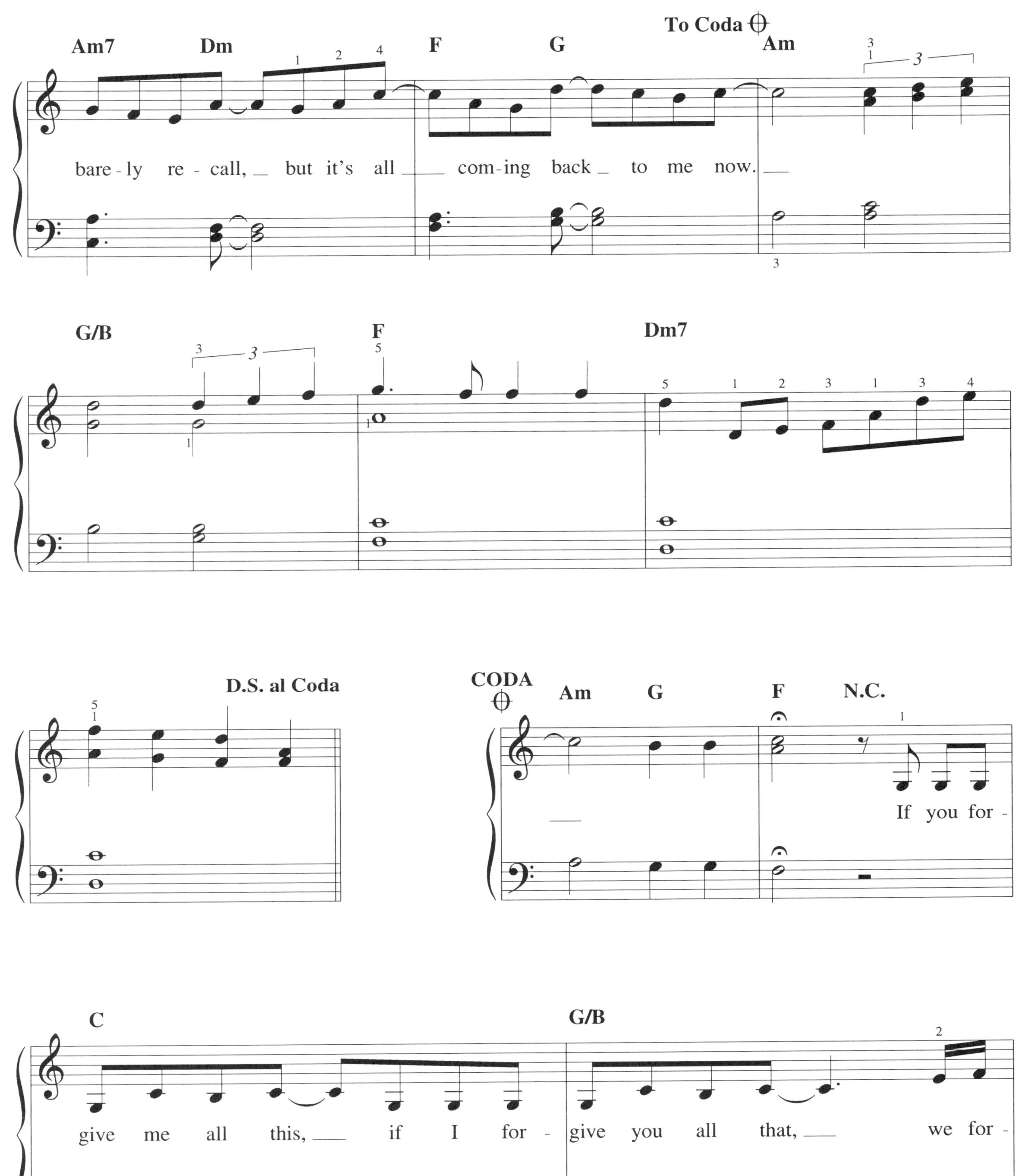
To Coda
Am7
Dm
F
G
Am
bare-ly re-call, but it's all com-ing back to me now.
G/B
F
Dm7
D.S. al Coda
CODA
Am
G
F
N.C.
If you for-
C
G/B
give me all this, if I for-give you all that, we for-

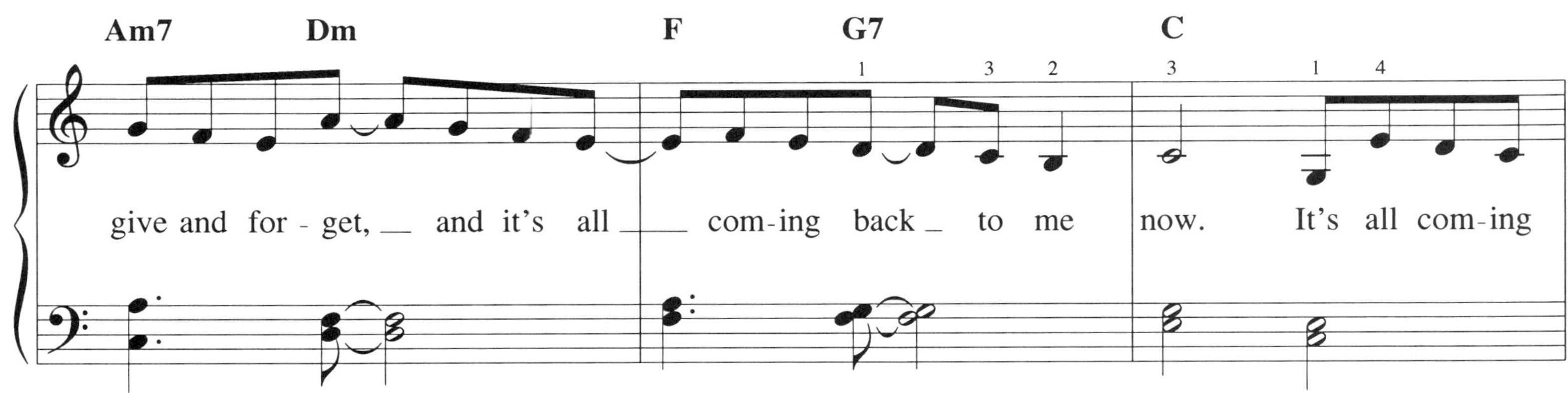
Am7
Dm
F
G7
C
give and for - get, and it's all com-ing back to me now. It's all com-ing

F
G
C
back to me now. And when I touch you like that, it's all com-ing

F
G
C
back to me now. And if you do it like this, it's all com-ing

F
C
back to me now. And if we...
rit.

WANNABE

Words and Music by MATT ROWE,
RICHARD STANNARD and SPICE GIRLS

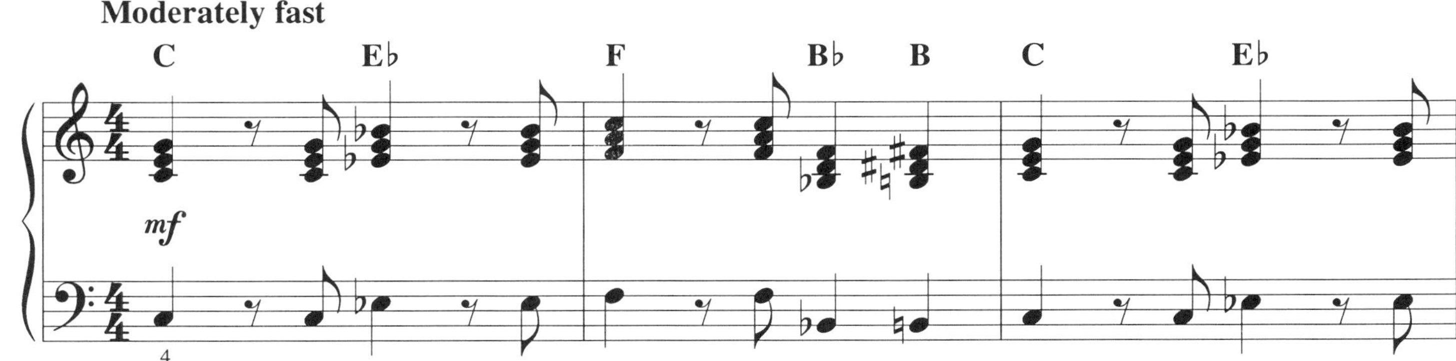

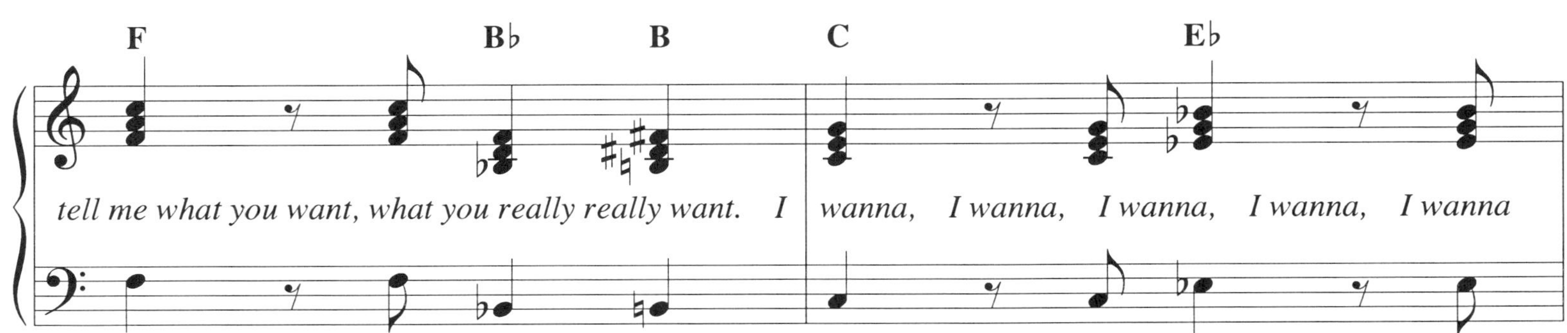

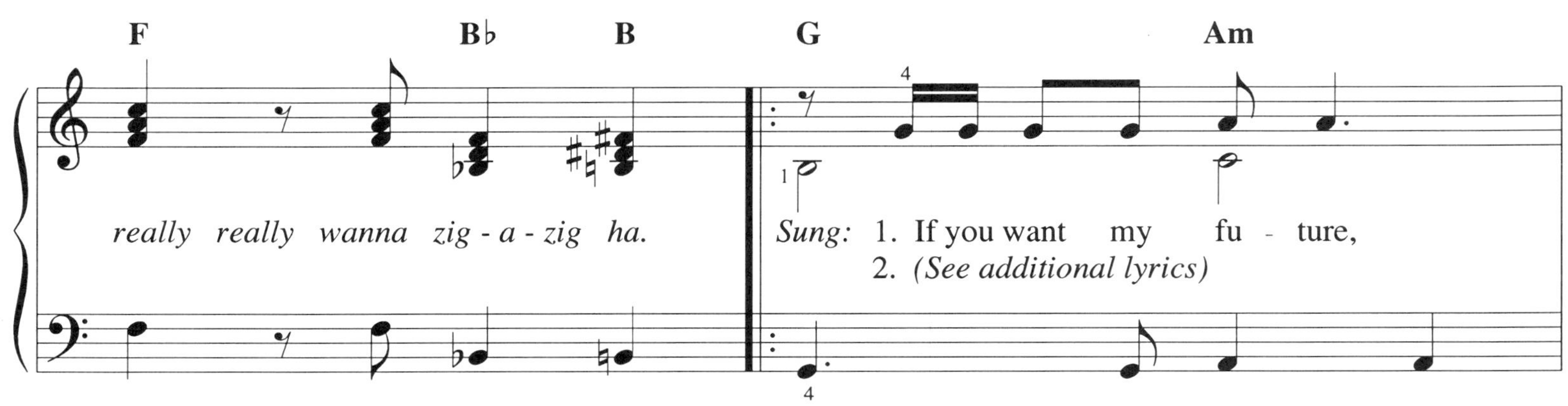
F
B♭
B
G
Am
really really wanna zig - a - zig ha.
Sung: 1. If you want my fu - ture,
2. (See additional lyrics)

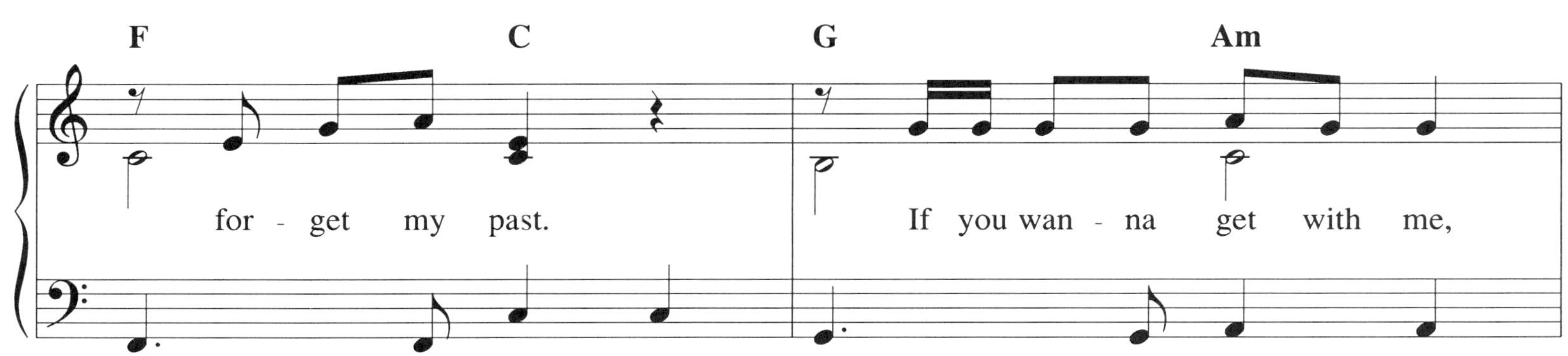
F
C
G
Am
for - get my past.
If you wan - na get with me,

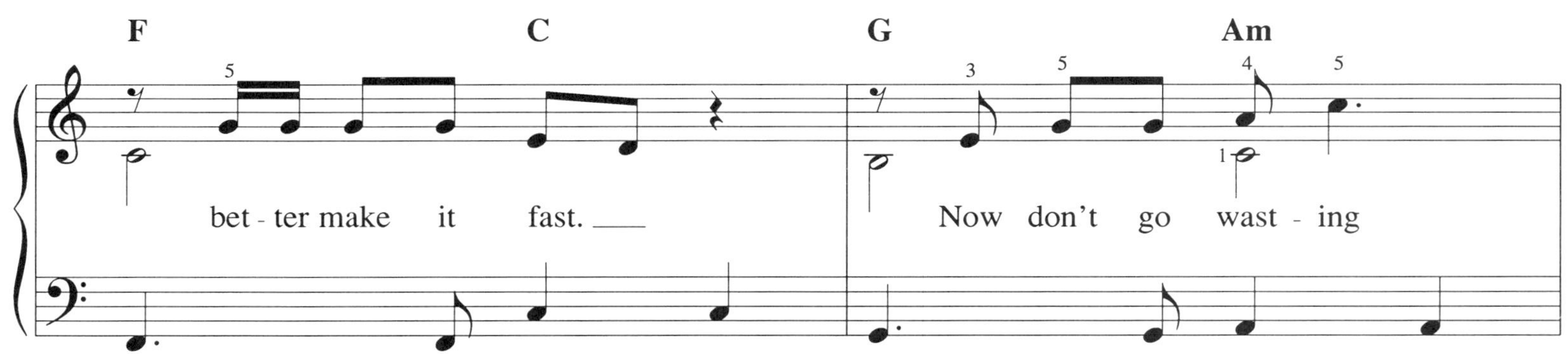
F
C
G
Am
bet - ter make it fast.
Now don't go wast - ing

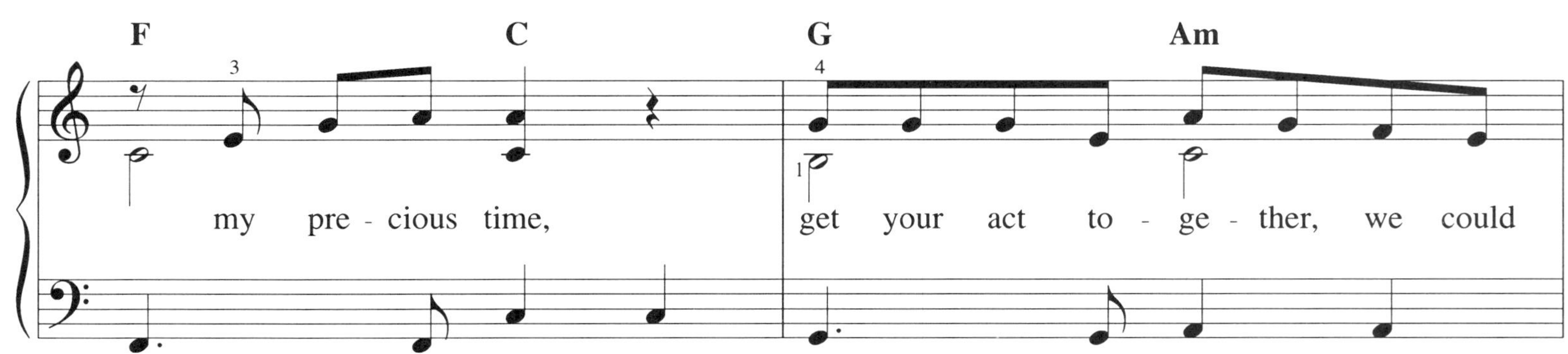
F
C
G
Am
my pre - cious time,
get your act to - ge - ther, we could

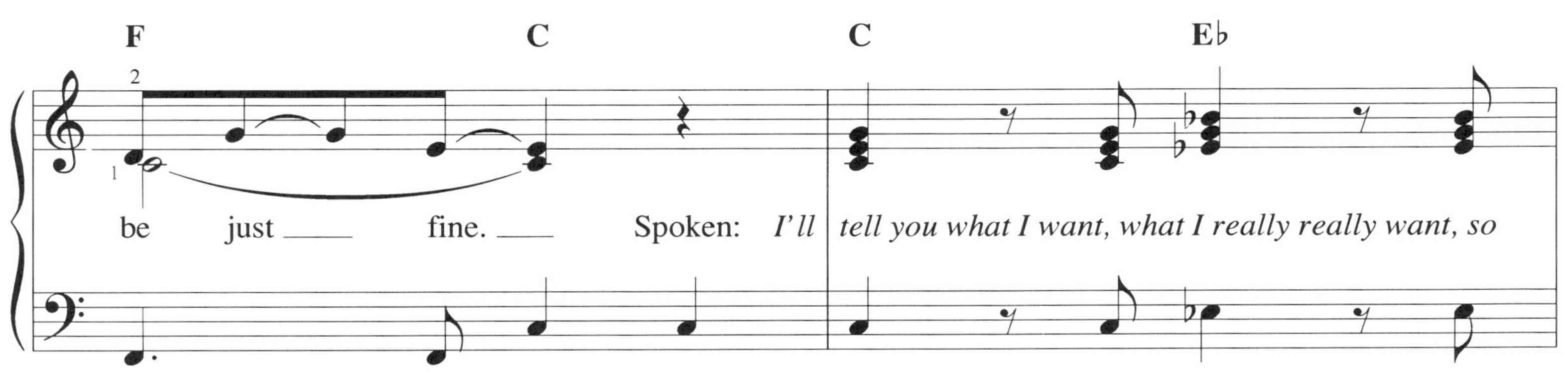
F
C
C
E♭
be just fine. Spoken: I'll tell you what I want, what I really really want, so

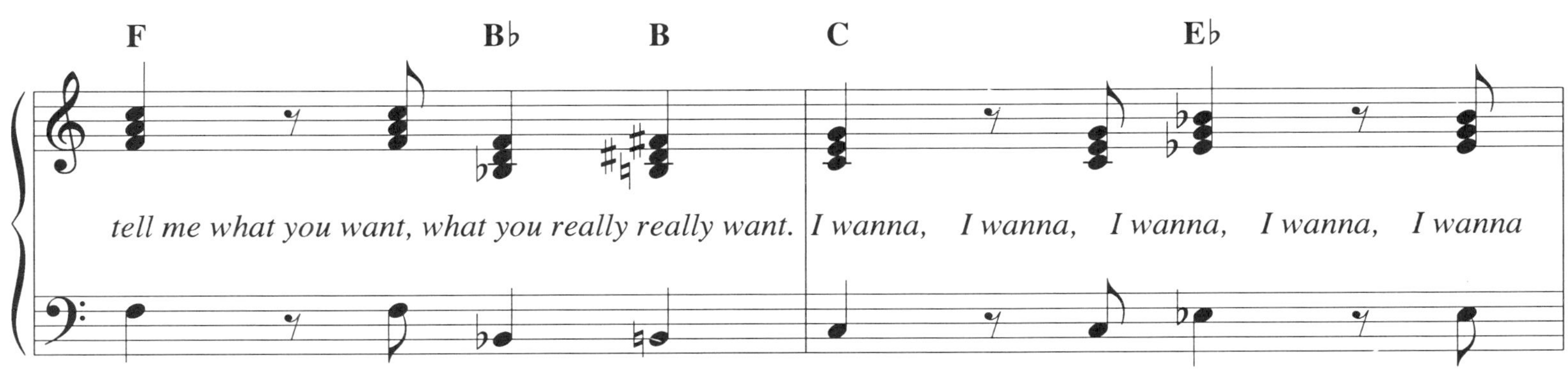
F
B♭
B
C
E♭
tell me what you want, what you really really want. I wanna, I wanna, I wanna, I wanna, I wanna

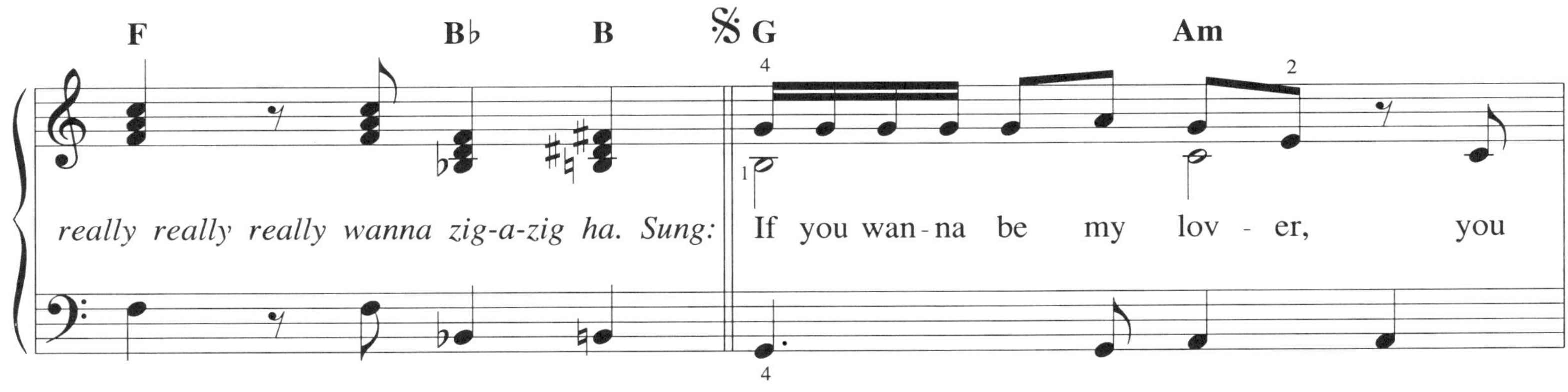
F
B♭
B
G
Am
really really really wanna zig-a-zig ha. Sung: If you wan-na be my lov - er, you

F
C
G
Am
got - ta get with my friends. Make it last for - ev - er, friend -

F
C
G
Am
- ship nev - er ends.
If you wan - na be my lov - er

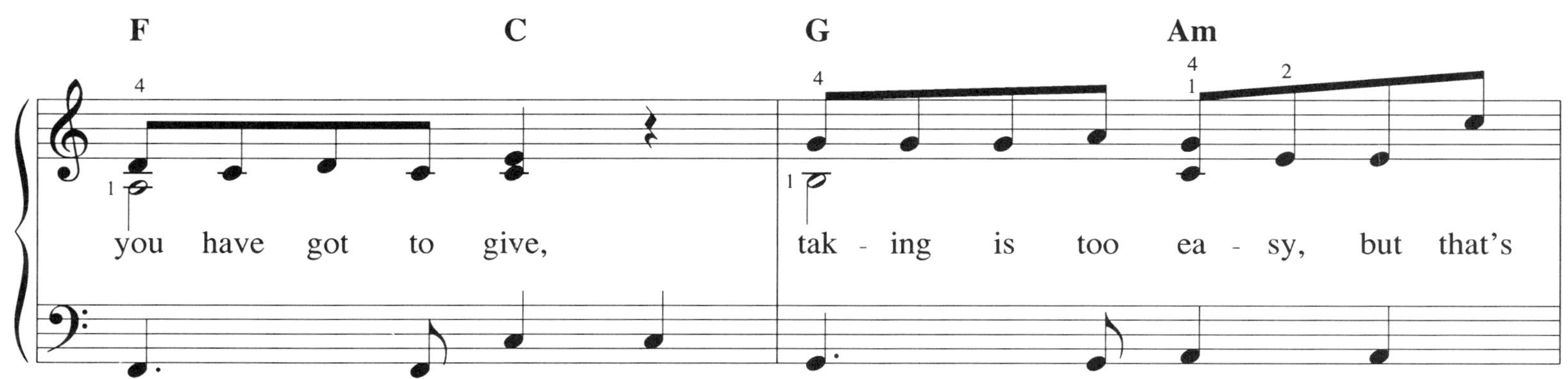
F
C
G
Am
you have got to give,
tak - ing is too ea - sy, but that's

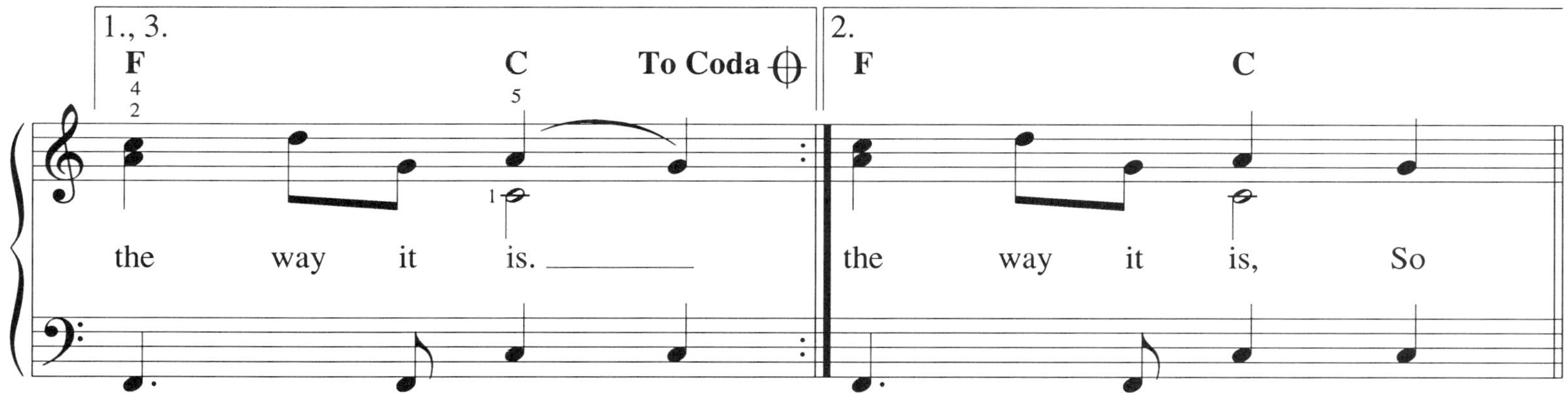
1., 3.
F
C
To Coda
2.
F
C
the way it is.
the way it is, So

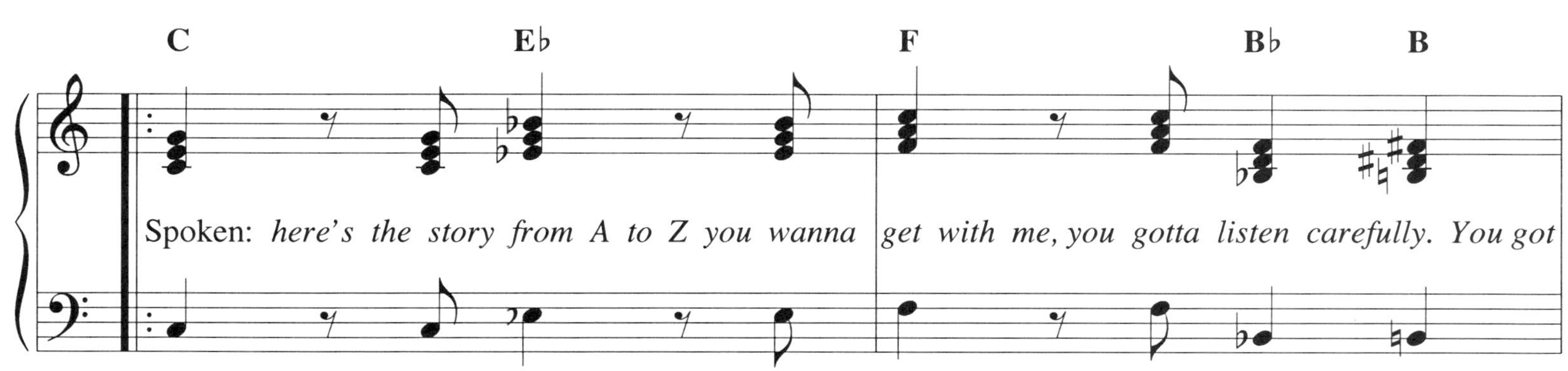
C
E♭
F
B♭
B
Spoken: here's the story from A to Z you wanna get with me, you gotta listen carefully. You got

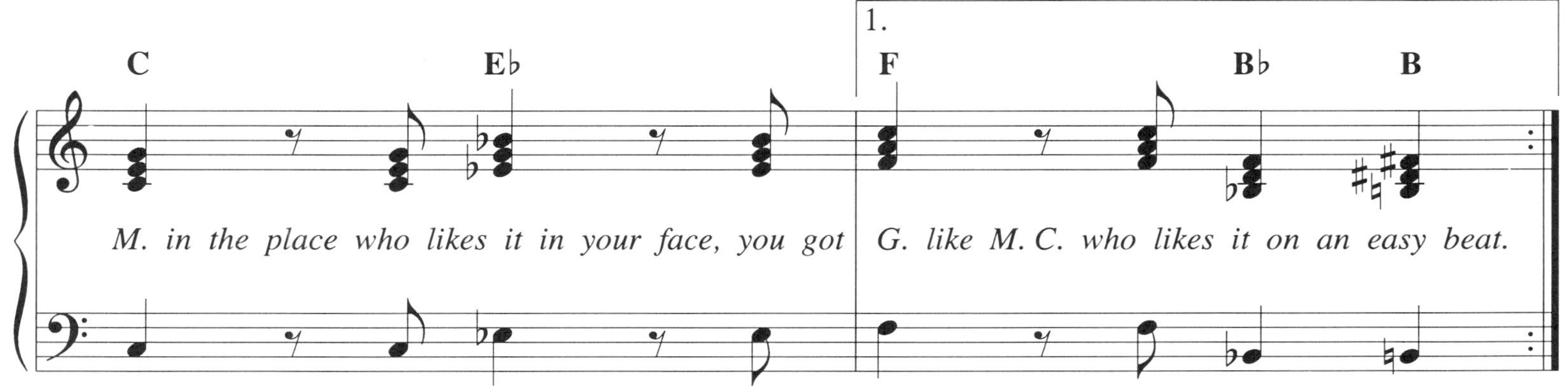

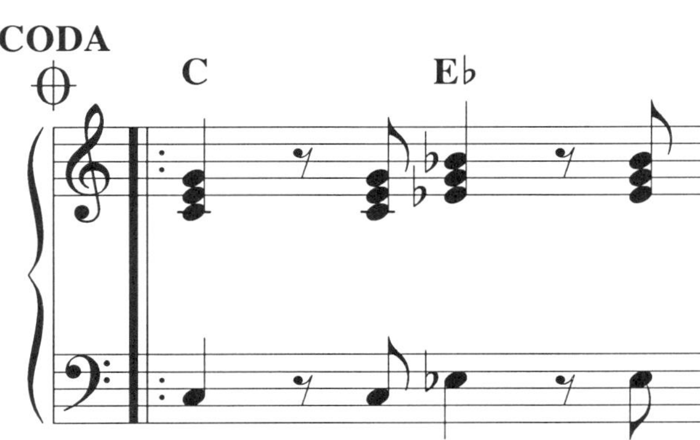

Additional Lyrics

2. What do you think about that now you know how I feel
Say you can handle my love, are you for real?
I won't be hasty, I'll give you a try
If you really bug me then I'll say goodbye.

YOU WERE MEANT FOR ME

Words and Music by JEWEL KILCHER
and STEVE POLTZ

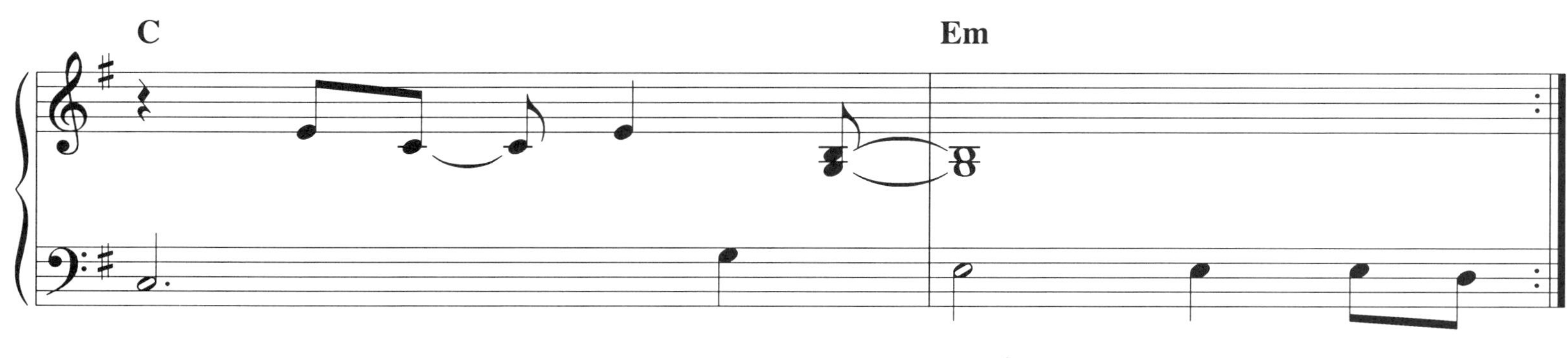

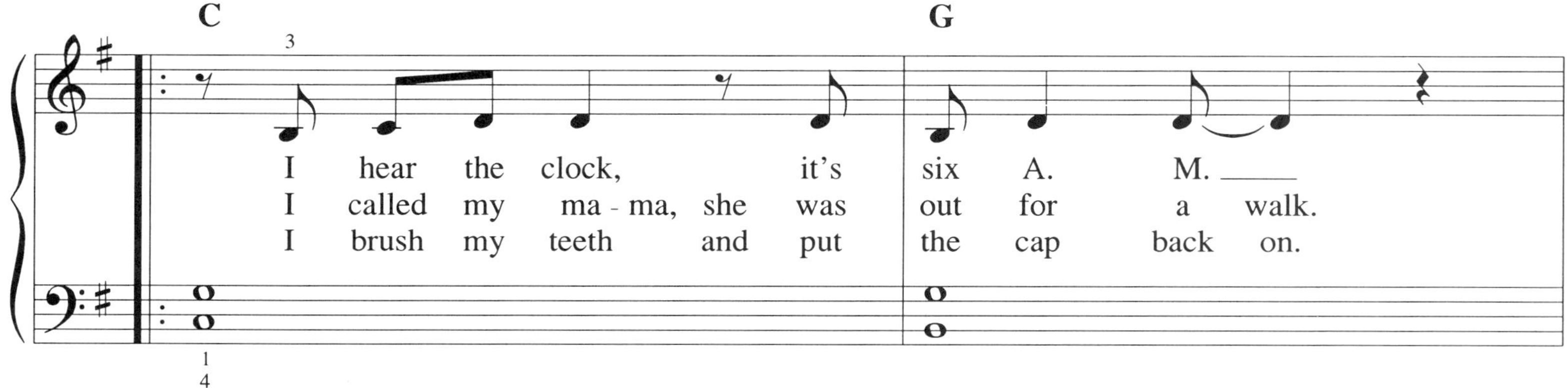

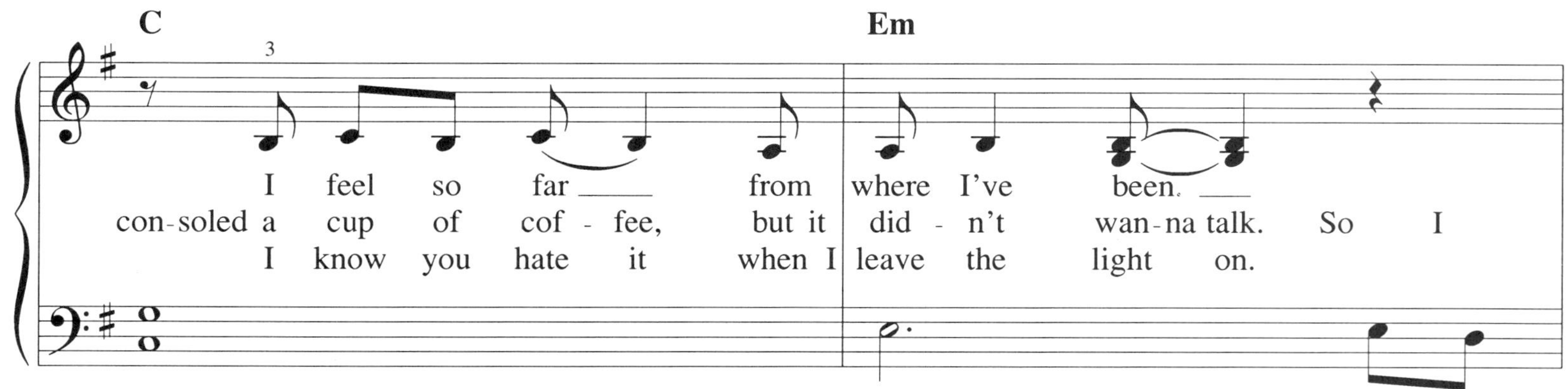

C
G
I've got my eggs, I've got my pan - cakes, too. I've
picked up a pa - per, it was more bad news. More
I pick a book up and then I turn the sheets down, and then I

C
D
3
3
3
got my ma - ple syr - up, ev - 'ry - thing but you.
hearts be - ing bro - ken or peo - ple be - ing used.
take a deep breath and a good look a - round.

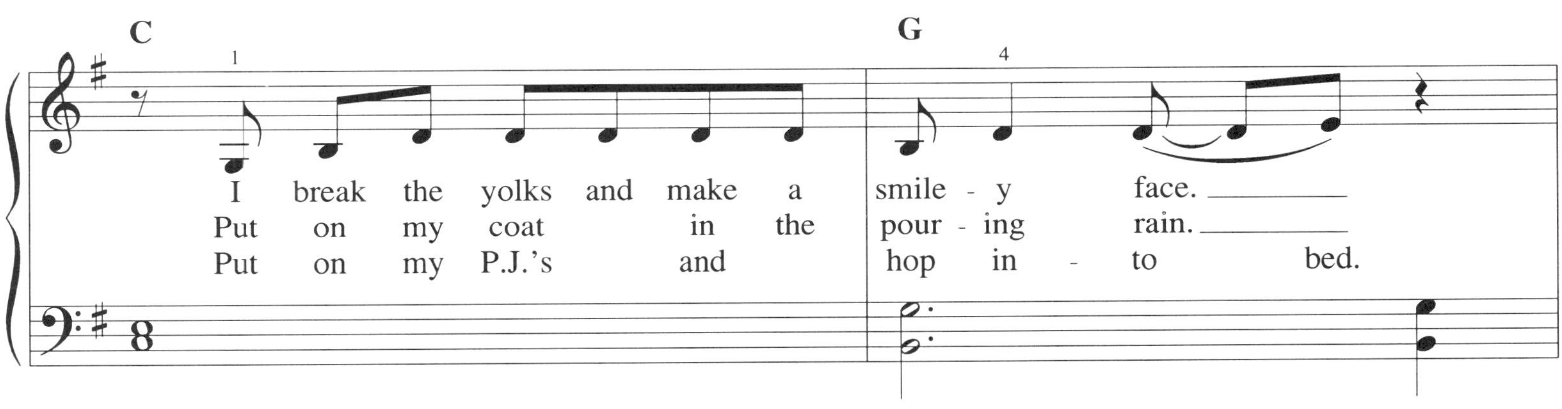
C
G
1
4
I break the yolks and make a smile - y face.
Put on my coat in the pour - ing rain.
Put on my P.J.'s and hop in - to bed.

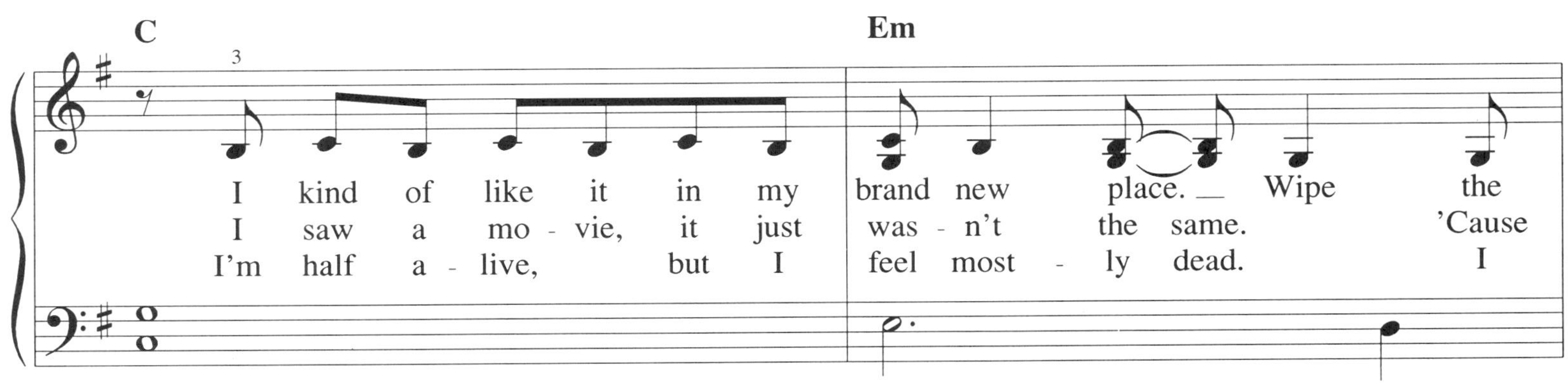
C
Em
3
I kind of like it in my brand new place. Wipe the
I saw a mo - vie, it just was - n't the same. 'Cause
I'm half a - live, but I feel most - ly dead. I

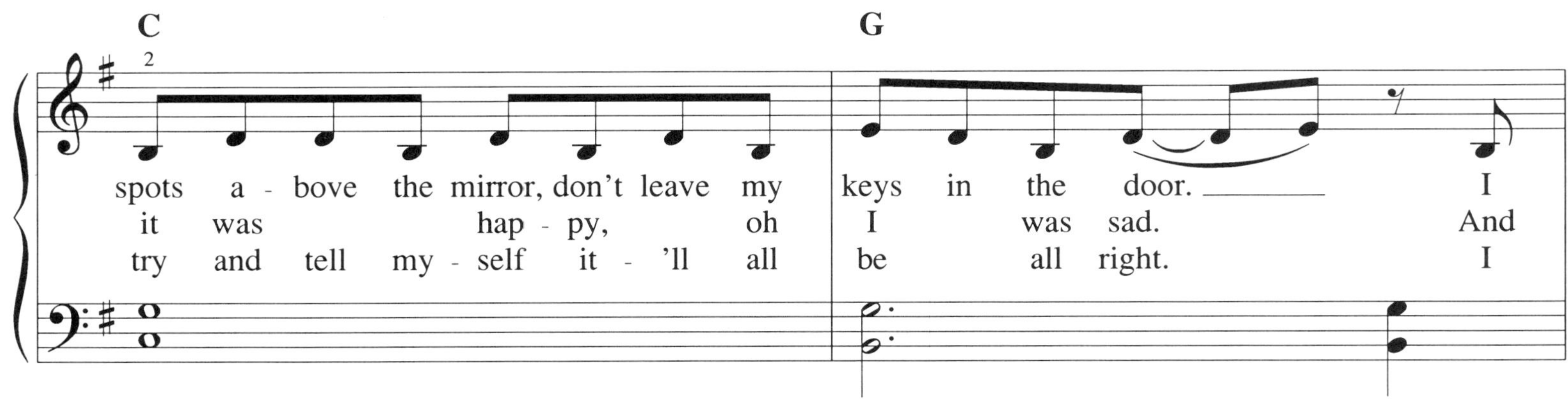
C
G
spots a - bove the mirror, don't leave my keys in the door. I
it was hap - py, oh I was sad. And
try and tell my - self it - 'll all be all right. I

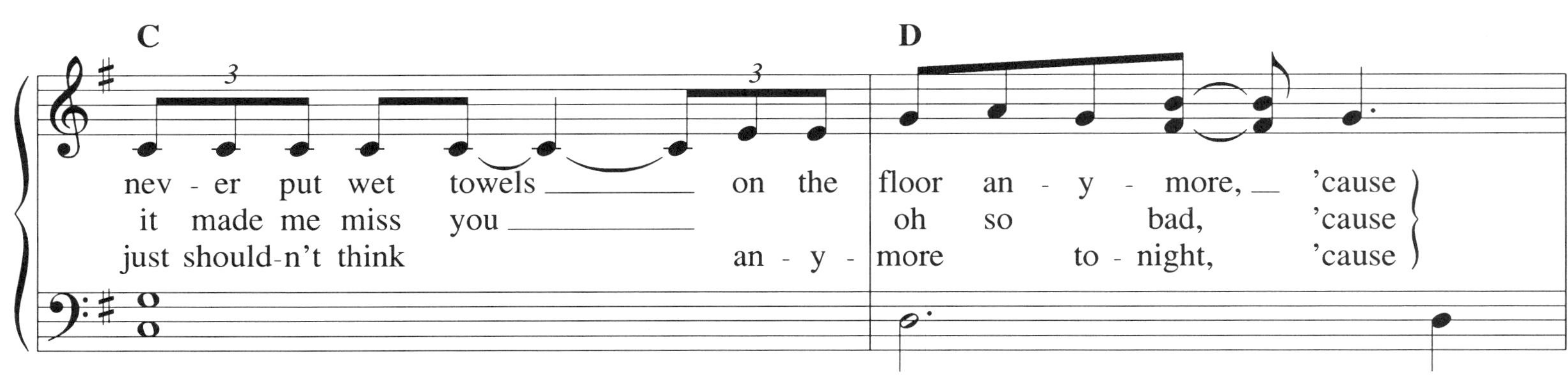
C
D
nev - er put wet towels on the floor an - y - more, 'cause
it made me miss you oh so bad, 'cause
just should-n't think an - y - more to - night, 'cause

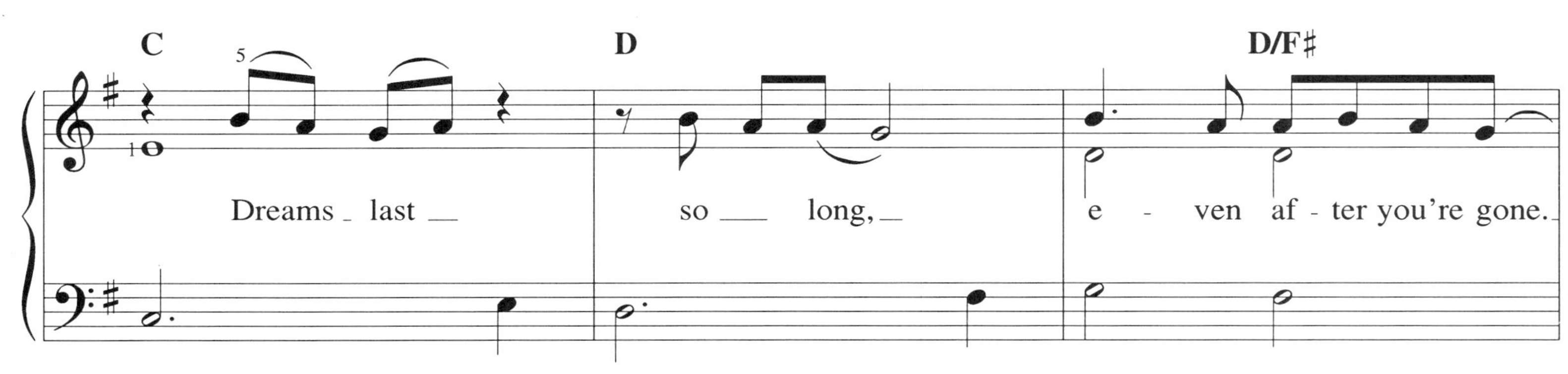
C
D
D/F♯
Dreams last so long, e - ven af - ter you're gone.

Em7
G/D
C
D
I know that you love me and

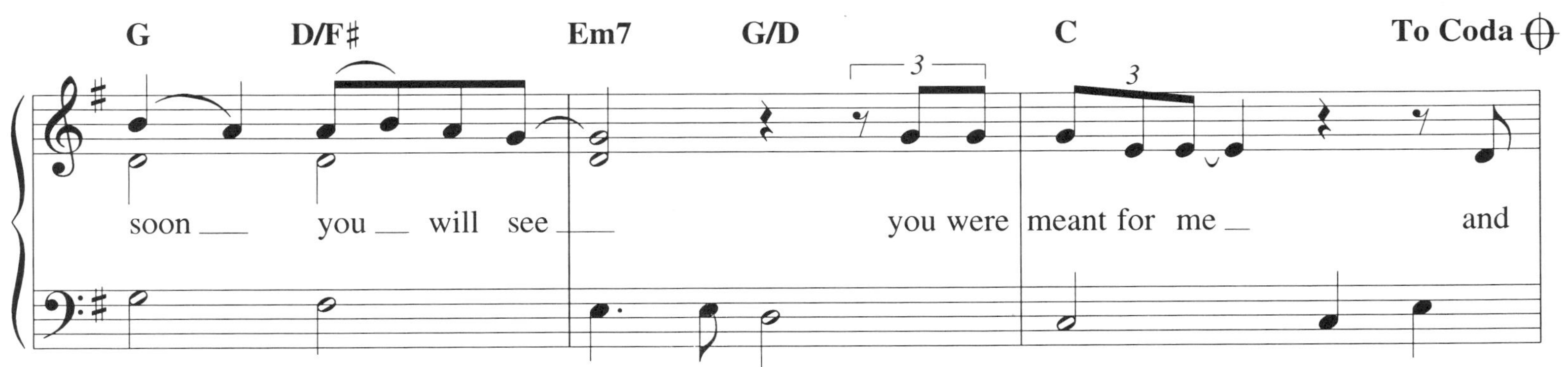
G
D/F♯
Em7
G/D
C
To Coda
soon you will see you were meant for me and

1.
D
Em
D
I was meant for you.

2.
D
Em
I was meant for you. I

Am7
D
go a - bout my bus - 'ness, I'm do - in' fine. Be - sides,

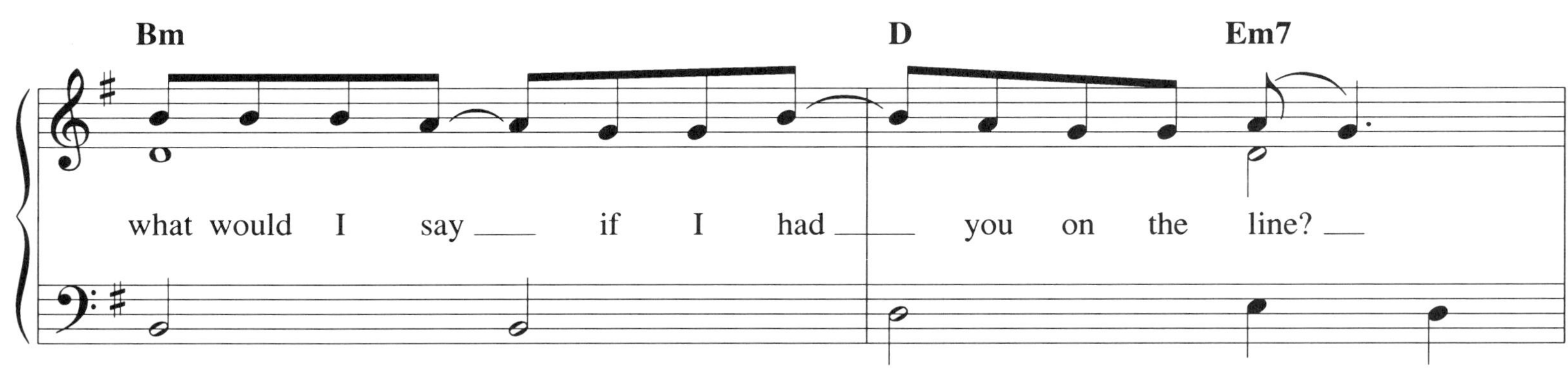
Bm
D
Em7
what would I say if I had you on the line?

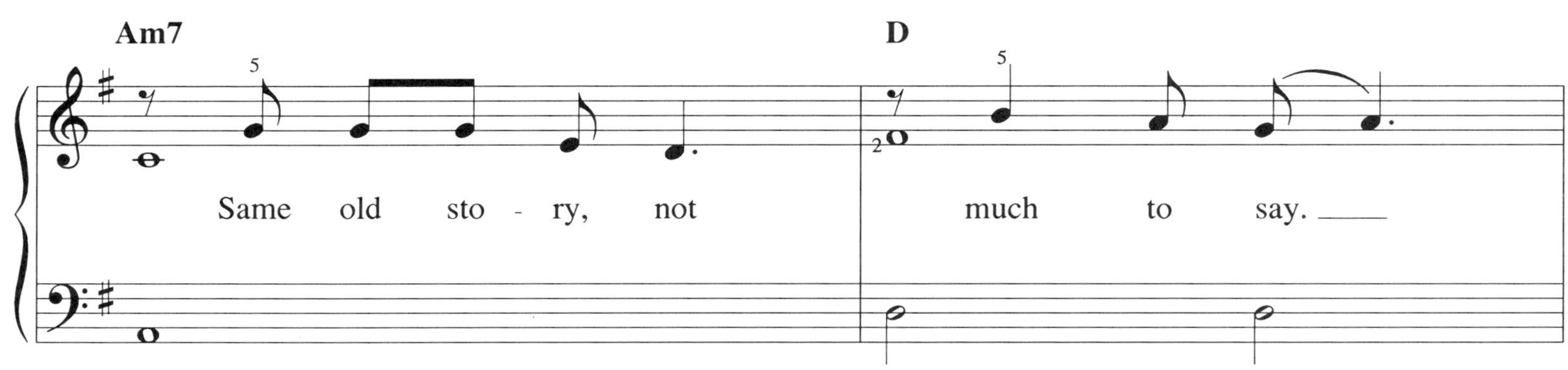
Am7
D
Same old sto - ry, not much to say.

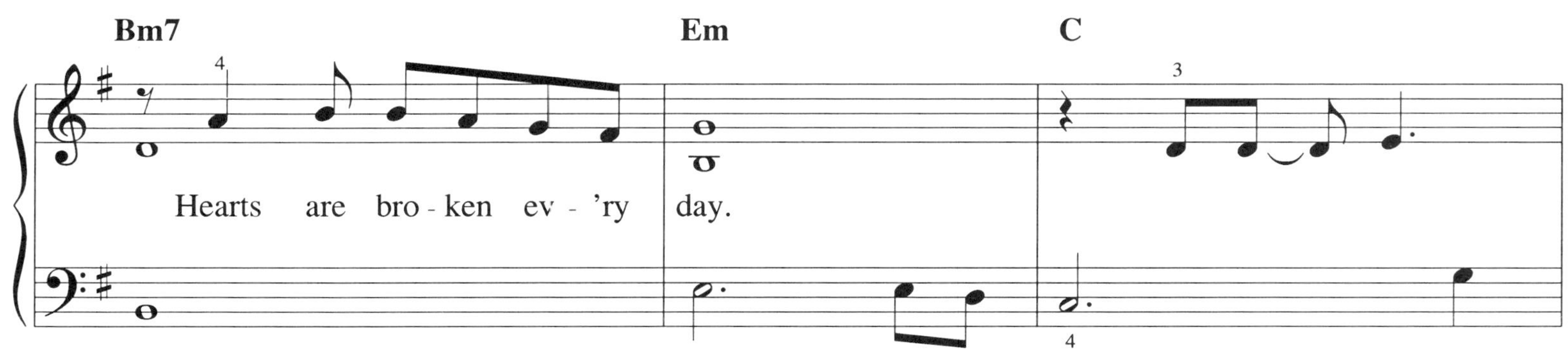
Bm7
Em
C
Hearts are bro - ken ev - 'ry day.

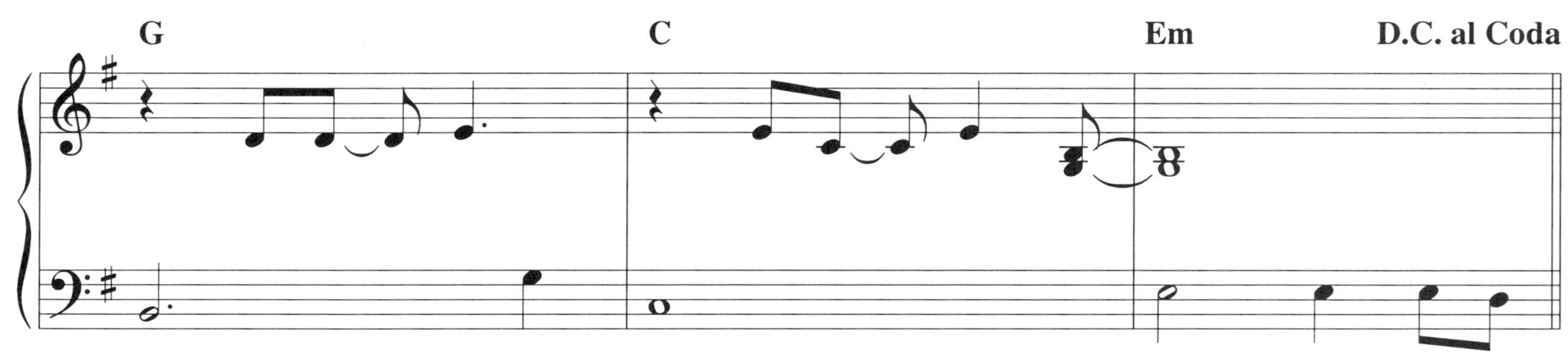
G
C
Em
D.C. al Coda

CODA
D
Em
I was meant for you.
Yeah, you were meant for me and
C
D
C
I was meant for you.
G
C
Em
rit.

YOU MUST LOVE ME

from the Cinergi Motion Picture EVITA

Words by TIM RICE
Music by ANDREW LLOYD WEBBER

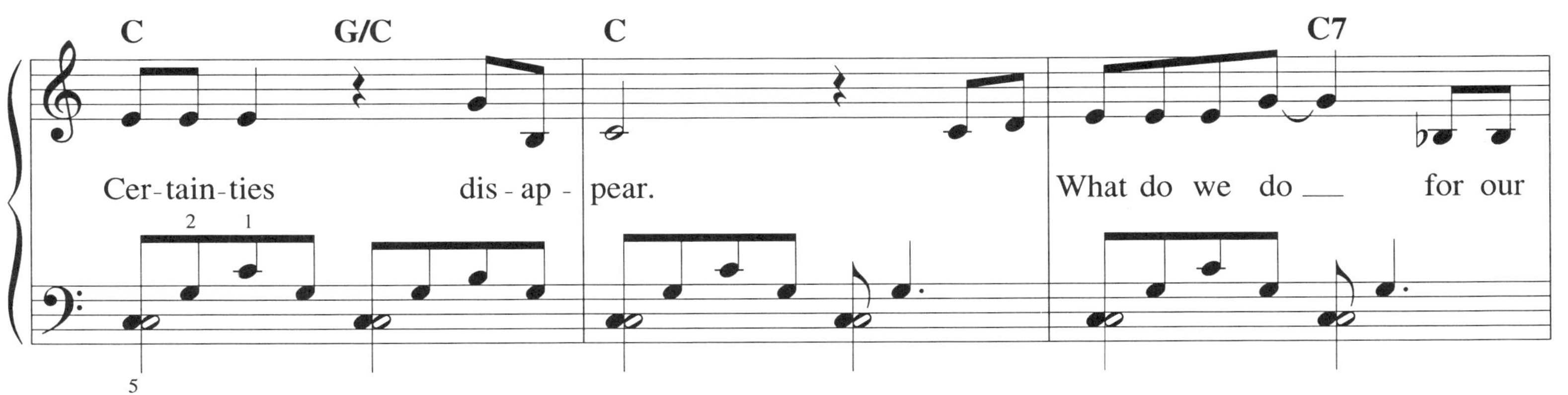
C G/C C C7
Cer-tain-ties dis-ap-pear. What do we do for our

F Dm7
dream to sur-vive, how do we keep all our pas-sions a-live as

F/G G F/G G E7
we used to do? Deep in my heart I'm con-

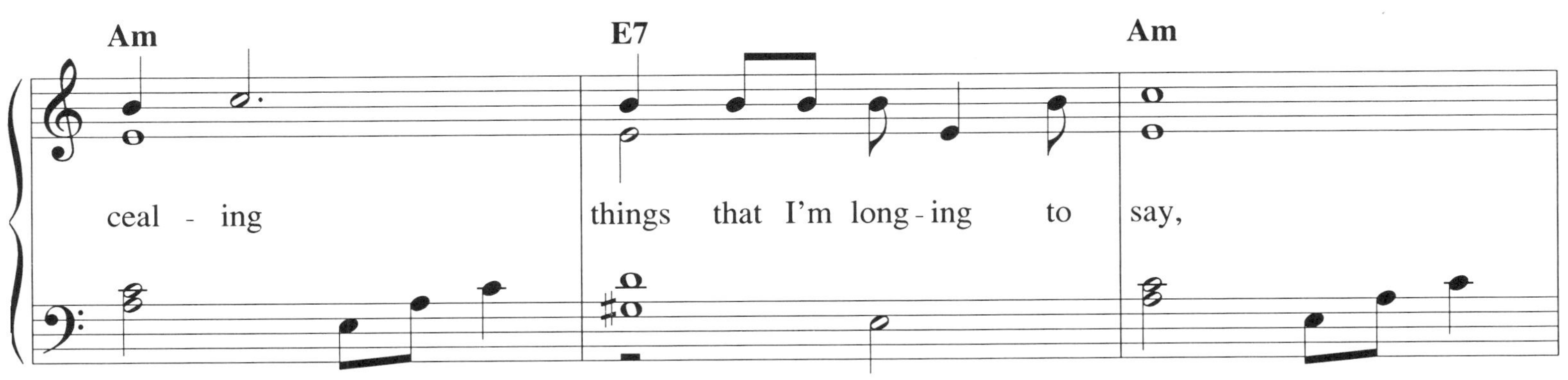
Am E7 Am
ceal-ing things that I'm long-ing to say,

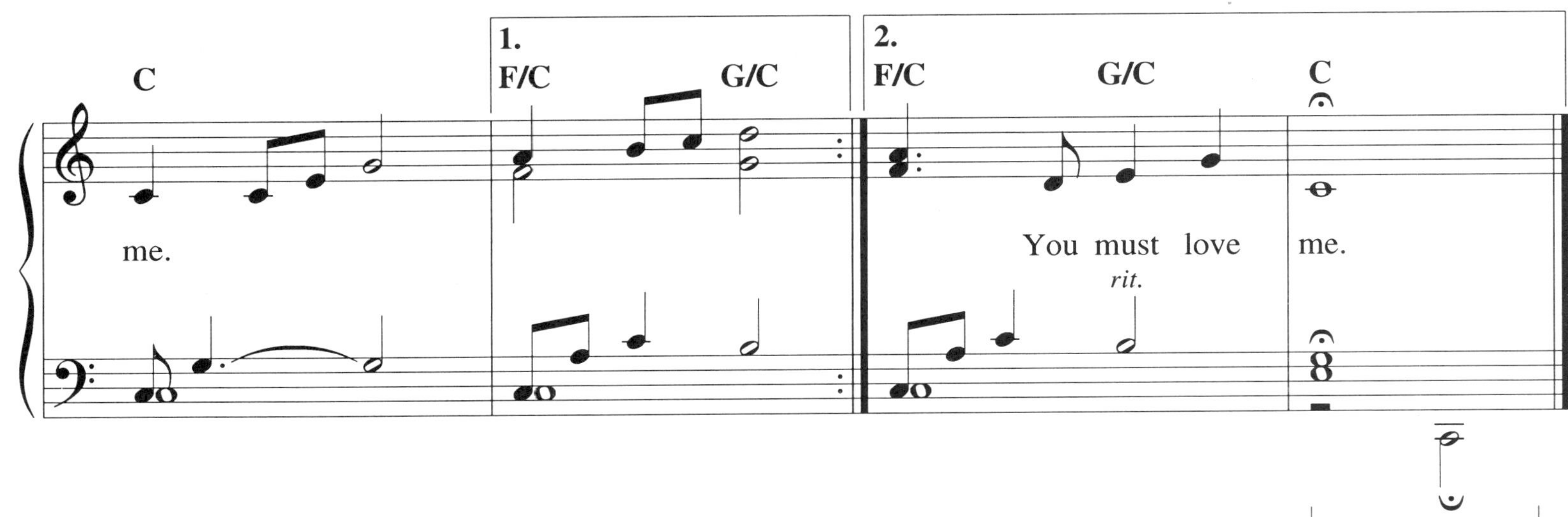

Additional Lyrics

Verse 2: *(Instrumental 8 bars)*
Why are you at my side?
How can I be any use to you now?
Give me a chance and I'll let you see how
Nothing has changed.
Deep in my heart I'm concealing
Things that I'm longing to say,
Scared to confess what I'm feeling
Frightened you'll slip away,
You must love me.